TAO TEH KING

By the same author

Philosophy of the Buddha, 1958, 1962, 1969, 1982

The World's Living Religions, 1964, 1971, 1992

The Heart of Confucius, 1969, 1971, 1977

Bhagavad Gita; The Wisdom of Krishna, 1970

Comparative Philosophy, 1977

The Philosopher's World Model, 1979

Why Be Moral? 1992

TAO TEH KING

BY

LAO TZU

Interpreted as

NATURE AND INTELLIGENCE

by

ARCHIE J. BAHM
Professor of Philosophy, University of New Mexico

SECOND EDITION
WORLD BOOKS

Albuquerque

To Luna

FOREWORD

The *Tao Teh King* speaks for itself far better than anything which may be said about it. The doctrine is so simple, clear and obvious that it is its own best introduction. Hence the text is placed first in this volume.

Readers unfamiliar with Oriental thought who may wish some assistance in understanding a view so often presented as mysterious, foreign, ancient, profound and obscure may refer to the summaries and comparisons following the text.

CONTENTS

Tao Teh King   11

Comments by the Author   71

Bibliography   121

Acknowledgments   131

TAO TEH KING

I

Nature can never be completely described, for such a description of Nature would have to duplicate Nature.

No name can fully express what it represents.

It is Nature itself, and not any part (or name or description) abstracted from Nature, which is the ultimate source of all that happens, all that comes and goes, begins and ends, is and is not.

But to describe Nature as "the ultimate source of all" is still only a description, and such a description is not Nature itself. Yet since, in order to speak of it, we must use words, we shall have to describe it as "the ultimate source of all."

If Nature is inexpressible, he who desires to know Nature as it is in itself will not try to express it in words.

To try to express the inexpressible leads one to make distinctions which are unreal.

Although the existence of Nature and a description of that existence are two different things, yet they are also the same.

For both are ways of existing. That is, a description of existence must have its own existence, which is different from the existence of that which it describes; and so again we have to recognize an existence which cannot be described.

II

It is because we single out something and treat it as distinct from other things that we get the idea of its opposite. Beauty, for example, once distinguished, suggests its opposite, ugliness.

And goodness, when we think of it, is naturally opposed to badness.

In fact, all distinctions naturally appear as opposites. And opposites get their meaning from each other and find their completion only through each other. The meanings of "is" and "is not" arise from our distinguishing between them.

Likewise, "difficult and easy," "long and short," "high and low," "loud and soft," "before and after"—all derive their meanings from each other.

Therefore the intelligent man accepts what is as it is. In seeking to grasp what is, he does not devote himself to the making of distinctions which are then mistaken to be separate existences.

In teaching, he teaches, not by describing and pointing out differences, but by example.

Whatever is exists, and he sees that nothing is gained by representing what fully exists by a description—another lesser, diluted kind of existence.

If something exists which cannot be wholly revealed to him with his viewpoint, he does not demand of it that it be nothing but what it seems to him.

If some one else interprets him, he does not trust that interpretation as being equal to his existence.

If some part of him stands out as if a superior representative of his nature, he will not surrender the rest of his nature to it.

And in not surrendering the whole of his nature to any part of it, he keeps himself intact.

This is how the intelligent man preserves his nature.

III

If no distinctions of superiority and inferiority prevail among officers, they will devote themselves to their tasks rather than to rivalries with one another.

If no special value is placed upon rare things, one will have no incentive for stealing them.

If nothing appears to arouse envy, one will remain satisfied with things as they are.

Since this is so, the wise administrator does not lead people to set their hearts upon what they cannot have, but satisfies their inner needs.

He does not promote ambition to improve their status, but supports their self-sufficiency.

He does not complicate their lives with knowledge of multifarious details or with an urge to attend to this, that and the other.

By keeping people contented, he prevents those who mistakenly believe that ambition is better than contentment from leading the contented astray.

By being calm and contented himself, he sets an example for his people.

IV

Nature contains nothing but natures; and these natures are nothing over and above Nature.

In Nature, all natures originate, all conflicts are settled, all differences are united, all disturbances are quieted.

Yet, no matter how many natures come into being, they can never exhaust Nature.

To look for an external source of Nature is foolish, for Nature is the source of all else.

V

Opposites are not sympathetic to each other.

Each one of the many kinds of opposites acts as if it could get along without its other.

But Nature treats opposites impartially, dealing with each of every pair of opposites with the same indifference.

And the intelligent man will regard opposites in the same manner.

No matter how deeply natures are torn by opposition, Nature itself remains unchanged.

In conflicts between opposites, the more one attacks his seeming opponent (upon which he really depends for his completion), the more he defeats himself (and thereby demonstrates that only Nature, and not any opposite abstracted from existence, is self-sufficient).

So, likewise, no matter how much debaters argue, their argument proves nothing.

Things are what they are, regardless of how much we disagree about them.

VI

The tendency toward opposition is ever-present.

Opposition is the source of all growth.

And the principle of opposition is the source of all opposites.

The principle of opposition is inherent in Nature, so oppositeness will continue forever, no matter how many opposites may come and go.

VII

The principle of initiation persists; and the principle of completion continues also.

Why do such opposing principles persist? Because they inhere in Nature, rather than stand by themselves.

That is why opposites endure.

The intelligent man, when an issue arises, stands off and observes both contentions.

Since he does not take sides, he never loses a battle.

By not favoring one side more than another, he is able to appreciate the virtues of both sides.

VIII

The best way to conduct oneself may be observed in the behavior of water.

Water is useful to every living thing, yet it does not demand pay in return for its services; it does not even require that it be recognized, esteemed, or appreciated for its benefits.

This illustrates how intelligent behavior so closely approximates the behavior of Nature itself.

If experience teaches that houses should be built close to the ground,

That friendship should be based upon sympathy and good will,

That good government employs peaceful means of regulation,

That business is more successful if it employs efficient methods,

That wise behavior adapts itself appropriately to the particular circumstances,

All this is because these are the easiest ways.

If one proceeds naturally, without ambition or envy, everything works out for the best.

IX

Going to extremes is never best.

For if you make a blade too sharp, it will become dull too quickly.

And if you hoard all the wealth, you are bound to be attacked.

If you become proud and arrogant regarding your good fortune, you will naturally beget enemies who jealously despise you.

The way to success is this: having achieved your goal, be satisfied not to go further.

For this is the way Nature operates.

X

If you would retain a wholesome personality, must you not restrain your lower interests from dominating over your higher interests?

If you wish to live healthily, should you not breathe naturally, like a child, and not hold your breath until your vitality is nearly exhausted?

If you desire to realize the potentialities of your indescribable original nature, how can you insist that some selected aspect of your personality is really superior to that original nature?

If you are required to govern others, ought you not be able to guide them by example, rather than by forcing your will upon them?

If Nature's way is a joint process of initiation and completion, sowing and reaping, producing and consuming, can you rightly demand that you deserve always to play the role of the consumer?

If you desire to know the natures of the various kinds of things, must you meddle with them, experiment with them, try to change them, in order to find out?

Nature procreates all things and then devotes itself to caring for them,

Just as parents give birth to children without keeping them as slaves.

It willingly gives life, without first asking whether the creatures will repay for its services.

It provides a pattern to follow, without requiring anyone to follow it.

This is the secret of intelligent activity.

XI

Every positive factor involves its negative or opposing factor; for example:

In order to turn a wheel, although thirty spokes must revolve, the axle must remain motionless; so both the moving and the non-moving are needed to produce revolution.

In order to mold a vase, although one must use clay, he must also provide a hollow space empty of clay; so both clay and the absence of clay are required to produce a vessel.

In order to build a house, although we must establish solid walls, we must also provide doors and windows; so both the impenetrable and penetrable are essential to a useful building.

Therefore, we profit equally by the positive and the negative ingredients in each situation.

XII

Interest in the varieties of color diverts the eye from regarding the thing which is colored.

Attention to the differences between sounds distracts the ear from consideration for the source of the sounds.

Desire for enjoyment of the various flavors misdirects the appetite from seeking foods which are truly nourishing.

Excessive devotion to chasing about and pursuing things agitates the mind with insane excitement.

Greed for riches ensnares one's efforts to pursue his healthier motives.

The intelligent man is concerned about his genuine needs and avoids being confused by dazzling appearances.

He wisely distinguishes the one from the other.

XIII

Pride and shame cause us much fearful anxiety.

But our inner peace and distress should be our primary concerns.

Why do pride and shame cause us so much fearful anxiety?

Because:

Pride attaches undue importance to the superiority of one's status in the eyes of others;

And shame is fear of humiliation at one's inferior status in the estimation of others.

When one sets his heart on being highly esteemed, and achieves such rating, then he is automatically involved in fear of losing his status.

Then protection of his status appears to be his most important need. And humiliation seems the worst of all evils.

This is the reason why pride and shame cause us so much fearful anxiety.

Why should our inner peace and distress be our primary concerns?

Because:

The inner self is our true self; so in order to realize our true self, we must be willing to live without being dependent upon the opinions of others. When we are completely self-sufficient, then we can have no fear of disesteem.

He who wisely devotes himself to being self-sufficient, and therefore does not depend for his happiness upon external ratings by others, is the one best able to set an example for, and to teach and govern, others.

XIV

Since what is ultimate in Nature cannot be seen with one's eyes, it is spoken of as invisible.

Since it cannot be heard with one's ears, it is called inaudible.

Since it cannot be grasped in one's hands, it is thought of as intangible.

But not even all three of these together can adequately describe it.

Nature did not originate in beginnings, and will not reach its goal in endings.

Rather it acts unceasingly, without either absolute beginnings or final endings.

If we cannot describe it intelligibly, this is because it is beyond our understanding.

Nature is the formless source of all forms, and yet it remains unaffected by its forms.

Thus it appears to us as if mysterious.

No matter how closely we scrutinize its coming toward us, we cannot discover a beginning.

No matter how long we pursue it, we never find its end.

One must comprehend the way in which the original Nature itself operates, if he wishes to control present conditions.

That is, he should study the ultimate source itself.

This is the way to understand how Nature behaves.

XV

In primitive times, intelligent men had an intuitively penetrating grasp of reality which could not be stated in words.

Since their instinctive beliefs have not been recorded for us, we can only infer them from old sayings which have come down to us.

Regarding caution when crossing a stream in winter: the more nervous you are, the more likely you are to slip and fall.

Regarding suspicion of enemies: the more you fear others, the more they will be afraid of you.

Regarding courtesy as a guest: the longer you stay, the more you become indebted to your host.

Regarding melting ice: the more you do to prevent it from melting, the quicker it melts.

Regarding making furniture: the more you carve the wood, the weaker it gets.

Regarding digging ditches: the steeper you slope their sides, the sooner they will wash down.

Regarding muddy water: the more you try to stir the dirt out of it, the murkier it gets.

What, then, should we do in order to clear the muddy water? Leave it alone and the dirt will settle out by itself.

What, then, must we do in order to achieve contentment? Let each thing act according to its own nature, and it will eventually come to rest in its own way.

Those who fully comprehend the true nature of existence do not try to push things to excess.

And because they do not try to push things to excess, they are able to satisfy their needs repeatedly without exhausting themselves.

XVI

In order to arrive at complete contentment, restrain your ambitions.

For everything which comes into being eventually returns again to the source from which it came.

Each thing which grows and develops to the fullness of its own nature completes its course by declining again in a manner inherently determined by its own nature.

Completing its life is as inevitable as that each thing shall have its own goal.

Each thing having its own goal is necessary to the nature of things.

He who knows that this is the ultimate nature of things is intelligent; he who does not is not.

Being intelligent, he knows that each has a nature which is able to take care of itself. Knowing this, he is willing that each thing follow its own course.

Being willing to let each thing follow its own course, he is gracious. Being gracious, he is like the source which graciously gives life to all.

Being like the gracious source of all, he embodies Nature's way within his own being. And in thus embodying Nature's way within himself, he embodies its perpetually recurrent principles within himself.

And so, regardless of what happens to his body, there is something about him which goes on forever.

XVII

The most intelligent leaders bring about results without making those controlled realize that they are being influenced.

The less intelligent seek to motivate others by appeals to loyalty, honor, self-interest, and flattery.

Those still less intelligent employ fear by making their followers think they will not receive their rewards.

The worst try to force others to improve by condemning their conduct.

But since, if leaders do not trust their followers then their followers will not trust the leaders,

The intelligent leader will be careful not to speak as if he doubted or distrusted his follower's ability to do the job suitably.

When the work is done, and as he wanted it done, he will be happy if the followers say: "This is just the way we wanted it."

XVIII

When people try to improve upon, and thus deviate from, the way Nature itself naturally functions, they develop artificial codes of right and wrong.

When knowledge becomes highly abstract, men are deceived by mistaking abstractions for realities.

When instinctive family sympathies are replaced by rules for proper conduct, then parents become "responsible" and children become "dutiful."

When corruption replaces genuine benevolence in government, then loyalty oaths are demanded of officials.

XIX

Therefore—

If we ignore intricate learning and knowledge of petty distinctions, we shall be many times better off.

If we neglect to insist upon the formal proprieties of etiquette, our intuitive sympathies will return.

If we abolish opportunities for profiteering "within the law," incentive for political corruption will disappear.

If the foregoing three principles are unclear, then at least the following are understandable:

Simply be yourself.

Act naturally.

Refrain from self-assertiveness.

Avoid covetousness.

XX

If we stop fussing about grammatical trivialities, we will get along much better.

The difference between "Yes" and "Ya" is insignificant as compared with a genuine distinction like "Good" and "Bad."

Yet some people are as fearful of making a grammatical mistake as of committing a vital error.

How stupid to waste our lives in infinite details!

While others enjoy devoting themselves to ceremonious holiday celebrations, such as the spring festivals, I stay at home as unperturbed as a helpless babe.

So while others are feasting, I appear neglected.

Am I the one who is a misguided fool?

When every one else is exuberant, I continue to be disinterested.

When everyone else is alert to the niceties of etiquette, I persist in being indifferent.

I am as unconcerned as the rolling ocean, without a care to bother me.

While others behave like busybodies, I alone remain placid and resist arousement.

How can I withstand the pressure of public opinion? Because I am succored by Mother Nature herself.

XXI

Intelligence consists in acting according to Nature.

Nature is something which can be neither seen nor touched.

Yet all of the forms which can possibly be seen or touched are latent within it.

And all of the things that will actually be seen or touched are embedded as potentialities within it.

Deep in its depths are activating forces.

No matter how unplumbable the depths, these forces unfailingly sustain the world as it appears to us.

From the beginning until now, they have never ceased to express themselves in appearances.

How do I know all this to be so? It is intuitively self-evident, for every existing thing testifies to it, including what appears right here and now.

XXII

Submit to Nature if you would reach your goal.

For, whoever deviates from Nature's way, Nature forces back again.

Whoever gives up his desire to improve upon Nature will find Nature satisfying all his needs.

Whoever finds his desires extinguished will find more desires arising of their own accord.

Whoever desires little is easily satisfied.

Whoever desires much suffers frustration.

Therefore, the intelligent person is at one with Nature, and so serves as a model for others.

By not showing off, he is exemplary.

By not asserting that he is right, he does the right thing.

By not boasting of what he will do, he succeeds in doing more than he promises.

By not gloating over his successes, his achievements are acclaimed by others.

By not competing with others, he achieves without opposition.

Therefore the old saying is not idle talk:

"Submit to Nature if you would reach your goal."

For this is the only genuine way.

XXIII

Things which act naturally do not need to be told how to act.

The wind and rain begin without being ordered, and quit without being commanded.

This is the way with all natural beginnings and endings.

If Nature does not have to instruct the wind and rain, how much less should man try to direct them?

Whoever acts naturally is Nature itself acting.

So whoever acts intelligently is intelligence acting.

And whoever acts unintelligently is unintelligence in action.

By acting naturally, one reaps Nature's rewards.

So by acting intelligently, one achieves intelligent goals,

Whereas by acting unintelligently, one comes to an unintelligent end.

Those who do not trust Nature as a model cannot be trusted as guides.

XXIV

One who tries to stand on tiptoe cannot stand still.

One who stretches his legs too far cannot walk.

One who advertises himself too much is ignored.

One who is too insistent on his own views finds few to agree with him.

One who claims too much credit does not get even what he deserves.

One who is too proud is soon humiliated.

These, when judged by the standards of Nature, are condemned as "Extremes of greediness and self-destructive activity."

Therefore, one who acts naturally avoids such extremes.

XXV

There exists something which is prior to all beginnings and endings,

Which, unmoved and unmanifest, itself neither begins nor ends.

All-pervasive and inexhaustible, it is the perpetual source of everything else.

For want of a better name, I call it "Nature."

If I am forced to describe it, I speak of it as "ultimate reality."

Ultimate reality involves initiation of growth, initiation of growth involves completion of growth, and completion of growth involves returning to that whence it came.

Nature is ultimate, the principle of initiating is ultimate, and the principle of perfecting is ultimate.

And the intelligent person is also ultimate.

Four kinds of ultimates, then, exist, and the intelligent man is one of them.

Man devotes himself to satisfying his desires, fulfilling his purposes, realizing his ideals, or achieving his goals.

But goals are derived from aims.

And all aiming is Nature's aiming, and is Nature's way of being itself.

XXVI

Saneness or sobriety is more basic than frivolity.

Calmness or self-sufficiency is superior to being agitated.

Therefore the intelligent man, though he goes on a long journey, will never depart far from his means of conveyance.

No matter how exciting the distractions, he never submits to their lures.

What would happen if Nature were to act frivolously?

If it became frivolous, it would be deprived of its sanity.

If it became agitated, it would lose control of itself.

XXVII

The wise traveler has no need to retrace his steps.

The effective speaker does not need to repeat himself.

The generous trader needs no scales.

The self-closing door needs no bolt; for it will not open itself even though it is not forced to stay shut.

Things which go together naturally do not have to be tied; for they will not separate even without bonds.

Therefore the intelligent man expresses his beneficence to other men by accepting each man's own way as best for himself.

And he performs the same service for all other beings, for he willingly recognizes that, by following its own nature, each thing does the best that can be done for it.

This may be called the two-pronged lesson:

Bad men can learn from the good man's successes.

Good men can learn from the bad man's failures.

Whoever despises such teachers, whether good or bad, or who fails to appreciate such lessons,

Even though he may be a "walking encyclopedia," is really a misguided fool.

This is the secret of wisdom.

XXVIII

He who knows how to be aggressive, and yet remains patient, becomes a receptacle for all of Nature's lessons.

Being thus receptive, he continually reembodies intelligence, and recuperates his primal nature.

He who knows how to be brilliant, and yet remains demure, becomes the ideal which all things have as their ultimate goal.

Being thus the ideal, he actualizes the unending goal of existence, and reinstates his primordial condition of perfect self-sufficiency.

He who knows how to be proud, and yet remains humble, becomes the recipient of all of Nature's bounties.

Being thus receptive, he reintegrates intrinsic goodness, and restores primitive wholesomeness.

Intrinsic goodness, when devoted to varieties of uses, functions as instrumental value.

When the intelligent man employs instrumental values, he treats them as means to ends,

For he is concerned with the ultimate ends, never mistaking the means as ends in themselves.

XXIX

Whenever someone sets out to remold the world, experience teaches that he is bound to fail.

For Nature is already as good as it can be.

It cannot be improved upon.

He who tries to redesign it, spoils it.

He who tries to redirect it, misleads it.

Consider how Nature operates:

Some things precede while others follow.

Some things blow one way while some blow another.

Some things are strong while others are weak.

Some things are going up while others are going down.

Therefore, the intelligent man avoids both extremes, shunning excess in one way as well as in the other.

XXX

Whoever tries to help Nature run itself does not need to use force.

For force will be met with force, and wherever force is used, fighting and devastation follows.

After the battle come years of destitution.

He who is wise lets well enough alone.

He does not press a victory by further conquest.

When peace has been restored, he does not behave like an arrogant victor.

When security has been regained, he does not gloat like a conqueror.

When he gets what he needs, he does not destroy those who have been defeated.

Whenever he does something which he has to do, he does it without cruelty.

When things reach maturity, they decay of themselves.

So cruelty is unnatural.

Whoever acts unnaturally will come to an unnatural finish.

XXXI

Weapons have a negative value, for they create fear in others.

Therefore, the follower of Nature avoids them.

For when among intimates, one naturally prefers the gentler, more trusting, position on the left.

And when among enemies, one naturally jockeys for the more strategic position on the right.

Since weapons have a negative value, the intelligent man will have nothing to do with them if he can.

But when he is forced to use them, he does so with reluctance and restraint.

He does not admire conquest.

For, whoever desires to conquer desires to kill.

And whoever delights in murder, cannot inherit the earth.

When things go well, we signify this by honoring the position on the left.

When ills prevail, we symbolize this by giving precedence to the position on the right.

In military parades, the second in command, who is ordered to give orders, takes his place on the left,

While the first in command, who by himself undertakes to give orders, takes the right-hand position.

There is a significant similarity between fighting and funerals.

Just as the slaughter of many people should be accompanied by weeping and mourning,

So the positions in a victory parade should properly parallel those in a funeral procession.

XXXII

Nature is always indeterminable.

Although, in its original simplicity, it may appear to be helpless, no one else can tell it what to do.

If legislators and administrators could keep this in mind, everyone would obey their laws without enforcement.

When opposites supplement each other, everything is harmonious.

Without compulsion, each supports the other.

But when boundaries between opposites appear, then the boundary lines are marked out.

Once one begins to differentiate between one thing and another, how will he know where to stop?

To know when to stop making distinctions is to be free from error.

The true relationship of every determinate thing to Nature is reintegrative, like all the rivers and rivulets ever returning to their ocean.

XXXIII

He who knows much about others may be learned, but he who understands himself is more intelligent.

He who controls others may be powerful, but he who has mastered himself is mightier still.

He who receives his happiness from others may be rich, but he whose contentment is self-willed has inexhaustible wealth.

He who occupies a place provided for him by others may live a long life, but he who dwells in his own self-constituted place, even though he decays, is eternal.

XXXIV

Ultimate reality is all-pervasive; it is immanent everywhere.

All other things owe their existence to it and draw their sustenance from it, without anyone being refused.

Having created and nurtured them, it does not demand title to them.

Even though it has provided for all, it refuses to dominate over a single one.

Since it asks nothing in return for its services, it may appear as of little worth.

But all things return home to it again, even though they do not know that they are being called home.

Therefore it may be thought of as ultimate.

Since it never claims ultimacy for itself, it is, by that very fact, ultimate indeed.

XXXV

He who grasps the ultimate structure of reality draws everyone to him.

They approach him without being harmed, but find security, satisfaction, and contentment.

Particular goods of various kinds attract the interests of men as they travel through life.

But the all-pervasive way of Nature attracts no attention to itself (for its true nature is not to be found in particulars).

Even though it is present in the mouth, it remains untasted.

Even though it is embodied in all objects, it remains unseen.

Even though it permeates sound, it remains unheard.

Yet, no matter how much we use it, it can never be exhausted.

XXXVI

The purpose of contracting (returning to Nature) is served by expanding (emerging out of Nature in the first place).

The purpose of weakening (subsiding or satisfying of desire) is served by strengthening (arousing the will to live).

The purpose of decline (of individual self-assertion) is served by arising (of individuality).

The purpose of taking away (culminating or perfecting life) is served by being given (i.e., "the last of life for which the first was made").

This is the most penetrating insight into the way of life.

The giving in or finishing always triumphs over the starting out.

Just as a fish should not be taken out of water,

So a sword should never be taken from its scabbard.

XXXVII

Nature never acts, yet it activates everything.

If legislators and administrators would behave likewise, each thing would develop in accordance with its own nature.

Just as, when things develop, those which become passionate are restrained by that passionless one which activates them,

So the way to restrain men's passions is by dispassionate restraint.

And thus all passion will subside.

XXXVIII

Intelligent control appears as uncontrol or freedom.

And for that reason it is genuinely intelligent control.

Unintelligent control appears as external domination.

And for that reason it is really unintelligent control.

Intelligent control exerts influence without appearing to do so.

Unintelligent control tries to influence by making a show of force.

The generous giver gives because he wants to give.

The dutiful giver gives because he wants to receive.

Whenever a regulation is imposed from above, it is not willingly obeyed.

Then effort is used to enforce it.

But when Nature's spontaneous activity disappears, then intelligent action is called for.

But when intelligent action is unavailable, then intuitive generosity may be appealed to.

But when intuitive sympathy is lacking, principles of morality may be invoked.

But where morality is ineffective, laws are enacted.

But where law is enforced, spontaneous and sincere loyalty declines, and disintegration of the harmonious society sets in.

Thus valuing law as an end in itself results in minimizing fidelity to Nature itself.

Knowledge of law appears at once as a flowering of Nature's way and as the source of error.

Therefore the intelligent man adheres to the genuine and discards the superficial.

He keeps the fruit rather than the flower,

Naturally preferring the one to the other.

XXXIX

There are things which have always maintained their own self-activity.

The tendency to initiate is, by its self-activity, obviously self-originating.

The tendency toward completion is, by its self-activity, always self-perfecting.

The tendency to maintain integrity, by its self-activity, sustains integrity.

The tendency to oppose is, by its self-activity, sufficient for all opposition.

It is by self-activity that all things fulfill themselves.

So it is by self-activity that the world is governed.

Such is the extent of self-activity.

If the tendency to initiate were not clearly such, it would be ineffective.

If the tendency toward completion were not dependable, things would be chaotic.

If the tendency to maintain integrity were not persistent, things would disintegrate.

If the tendency toward opposition were not sustained, vitality would disappear.

If there were no self-activity, life would cease.

If self-activity did not govern, then disruption would set in.

The esteemed must depend upon others for their esteem, whereas the unesteemed are self-sufficient.

The high must depend upon the low for its foundation, whereas the low serves as its own foundation.

Therefore intelligent leaders consider themselves as independent, self-sufficient, and unesteemed.

For, must not the unesteemed be the basis for the esteemed?

Therefore the unesteemed are the ultimate in esteem.

One cannot be outstanding when he is alone, and he should not try to be so when he is with others.

XL

Nature alternates dynamically.

When it completes what it is doing, then it starts all over again.

All that is springs from such alternation.

XLI

When the intelligent man hears about Nature's alternating way, he seeks to embody it within himself.

The mediocre man sometimes accepts it and sometimes does not.

Unintelligent men scoff at it.

Yet this very scoffing at intelligence itself exemplifies Nature's way of alternation.

This is the reason for the old sayings:

Nature's brightest day fades into night.

Nature's most luxuriant growth ages toward decay.

Nature's smoothest plain erodes itself away into rough terrain.

Nature's most harmonious adjustment generates conflict.

Nature's most beautiful objects grow grim and ugly.

Nature's greatest prize soon becomes despised.

Nature's strongest power eventually weakens.

Nature's soundest supports gradually rot away.

Nature's squarest corners soon become rounded.

Nature's grandest structures sooner or later are destroyed.

Nature's loudest sounds are finally silenced.

Hence, Nature, although beyond comprehension and description,

Knows how to bring about, alternately, all initiating and completing.

XLII

Nature first begets one thing.

Then one thing begets another.

The two produce a third.

In this way, all things are begotten.

Why? Because all things are impregnated by two alternating tendencies, the tendency toward completion and the tendency toward initiation, which, acting together, complement each other

Most men dislike to be considered of no account, lowly, unworthy.

Yet intelligent leaders describe themselves thus.

For people are admired for their humility and despised for their pride.

There are many other ways of illustrating what I am teaching:

"Extremists reach untimely ends."

This saying may be taken as a good example.

XLIII

That which is most yielding eventually overcomes what is most resistant.

That which is not becomes that which is.

Acting without coercing or being coerced is best.

Guiding by example rather than by words or commands is most successful.

Such simple truths are so hard to understand.

XLIV

Esteem by others or self-esteem, which is better?

To value things or to value your self, which is better?

To have more or to have less, which is worse?

The more you have, the more you have to lose.

The more you value things, the less you value your self.

The more you depend upon others for esteem, the less you are self-sufficient.

He who knows how to discriminate wisely avoids danger,

And continues safely on his way.

XLV

What is most complete is still incomplete;

Yet it is as complete as it can be.

That which has achieved the most, still has the whole of its future yet to be achieved;

Hence it will not stop achieving.

Make a thing as straight as possible;

Yet it is still crooked or will become crooked.

Acquire the greatest skill;

And there will still be endless skill to be acquired.

Develop the greatest power of expression;

And there will be much that is unexpressed and inexpressible.

The same may be said about activity and passivity and cold and heat.

Only he who fully accepts these alternations is the best guide for all to follow.

XLVI

When what is natural prevails in human affairs, horses forced to train for racing are returned to the fertile pastures.

When artificiality prevails in human affairs, horses are trained for war and are restricted to walled enclosures.

There is no greater evil than desiring to change others— (to take from or give to others what they do not, of their own accord, want to give or take).

There is no greater misfortune than desiring to change oneself—being discontented with one's lot.

There is no greater vice than desiring to change things— (to possess, control or reconstruct their natures).

Only he who is satisfied with whatever satisfactions his own nature provides for him is truly satisfied.

XLVII

Without going out-of-doors, one can know all he needs to know.

Without even looking out of his window, one can grasp the nature of everything.

Without going beyond his own nature, one can achieve ultimate wisdom.

Therefore the intelligent man knows all he needs to know without going away,

And sees all he needs to see without looking elsewhere,

And does all he needs to do without undue exertion.

XLVIII

While day by day the overzealous student stores up facts for future use,

He who has learned to trust nature finds need for ever fewer external directions.

He will discard formula after formula, until he reaches the conclusion: Let Nature take its course.

By letting each thing act in accordance with its own nature, everything that needs to be done gets done.

The best way to manage anything is by making use of its own nature;

For a thing cannot function properly when its own nature has been disrupted.

XLIX

The intelligent man is not willful.

He accepts what others will for themselves as his will for them.

Those who appear as good, he accepts,

And those who appear as bad, he accepts;

For Nature accepts both.

Those who appear faithful, he accepts,

And those who appear unfaithful, he accepts;

For Nature accepts both.

The intelligent man treats every kind of nature impartially,

And wills good to one as much as another.

All people admire the intelligent man,

Because he regards them all as a mother regards her children.

L

It is natural for man to be born and to die.

And it is also natural for each of his parts to be born and to die and to evolve through its life cycle.

Why do men become so perturbed and anxious to prolong the life of each part when endangered?

The truth is that whatever is natural is good.

Since it is natural for man to die anyway, being assisted by horn or claw or spear in bringing about his death in no way endangers his nature.

No wild buffalo horn can change the course of Nature.

No tiger's claw can act unnaturally.

No soldier's spear can go against Nature.

Why? Because death is natural, but Nature cannot die.

LI

Nature produces things, and intelligence guides them.

Although different in kind, each thing has its own self-sufficient intelligence to direct it.

Nothing can fail to emulate Nature and intelligence by embodying them within its own life.

Such emulation is not demanded, but occurs of its own accord.

Nature originates and suckles, rears and develops, protects and provides for, and guides and perfects all things.

Whatever is produced, Nature accepts it for what it is.

However it behaves, Nature lets it follow its own way.

Whatever its fortune, Nature injects no external interference.

Such is Nature's marvelous sagacity.

LII

Nature, because it has mothered all, may be regarded as Mother Nature.

He who understands Mother Nature, understands her children.

But to avoid the children's mistakes, one should follow close to Mother Nature herself,

If throughout his life he desires a safe guide.

If one remains silent and keeps to himself, he will not fail to fulfill his life;

But if he gives advice and meddles in others' affairs, he invites trouble.

If you see what is small as it sees itself,

And accept what is weak for what strength it has,

And use what is dim for the light it gives,

Then all will go well.

This is called acting naturally.

LIII

Let us be intelligent and follow Nature itself.

Let us not stray.

Nature's way is simple and easy, but men prefer the intricate and artificial.

When they congregate in artistically engineered cities, and neglect their farms, their food supply is cut off.

When they bedeck themselves with ornaments and weapons, and display their fancy foods and rich properties, they thereby invite thievery.

This is acting unnaturally.

LIV

What is deeply rooted in Nature cannot be uprooted.

He who embraces Nature's way as his own will not easily go astray;

And his children and grandchildren will continue to emulate him.

If one embodies Nature's way in his own life, he will be genuinely intelligent.

If he establishes it in his family, his home life will be felicitous.

If he cultivates it in his community, his future will be prosperous.

If he fosters it in his state, his future will be auspicious.

If he inspires it in the whole country, his benefit will become universal.

Thus one's own individual life serves as an example for other individuals.

One's family life serves as a model for other families.

One's community serves as a standard for other communities.

One's state serves as a measure for other states.

And one's country serves as an ideal for all countries.

How do I know all this?

It is obvious.

LV

He who is intelligent is like a little child.

Poisonous insects do not sting him.

Ferocious beasts do not attack him.

Wild birds do not claw him.

His bones are soft, his muscles weak, yet his grip is strong.

Because he has no urge for sexual union, he is fully satisfied.

His vitality is intact.

He can cry all day without getting hoarse.

His existence is harmonious.

To enjoy such harmony is to be in accord with Nature.

To be in accord with Nature is to be achieving the goal of life.

But to seek excitement is to invite calamity.

Those too eager for activity soon become fatigued.

For when things exhaust their vigor, they age quickly.

Such impatience is against Nature.

What is against Nature dies young.

LVI

He who is wise keeps silent;

He who advises is a fool.

The wise man shuts his mouth,

Closes his doors,

Curbs his anxieties,

Withdraws from entanglements,

Remains untempted by attractions,

And retains his self-sufficiency.

Nature is profoundly impartial.

It cannot be persuaded by pampering,

Nor dissuaded by scoffing.

It cannot be tempted by bribes,

Nor influenced by injury.

It cannot be cajoled by flattery,

Nor chagrined by slander.

Thus it is the most reliable thing in the world.

LVII

A good leader guides by good example;

A bad leader resorts to force and intrigue.

Everything gains by noninterference.

How do I know this?

Consider the evidence:

The more restrictions and taxes there are, the poorer the people become.

The more weapons people possess, the more they fight.

The more complicated machines become, the greater the danger from mechanical accident.

The more laws are enacted and taxes assessed, the greater the number of law-breakers and tax-evaders.

That is why the intelligent man concludes:

When I attend to my own business, other people are able to attend to theirs.

When I exemplify self-reliance, other people will devote themselves to the exercise of their own intelligence.

When I make no demands upon them, other people themselves will prosper.

When I express no desire to interfere in their lives, others will become genuinely self-sufficient.

LVIII

When government governs little, people are happy.

When government governs much, people are miserable.

Thus happiness depends upon little,

And misery depends upon much.

What does the desire to govern come to?

To restrict interferers is itself interference.

So attempts to increase happiness end only in misery.

Mankind has been foolish for so long a time!

The intelligent man knows what is best, but does not make others conform.

He knows directions, but does not direct.

He pursues the straightest way to the goal, but does not urge others to deviate from their course.

He is enlightened, but he cares not whether others see his light.

LIX

In managing men or anything else, the intelligent man uses self-restraint.

Only by self-restraint can one forestall trouble.

Forestalling trouble strengthens one's position.

Such strengthened position enables one to withstand everything.

Withstanding everything, one remains unchallenged.

Being unchallenged, one governs easily.

Because he embodies Mother Nature within himself, he retains a sound position.

This is the way to be deeply rooted and firmly based,

And durable and long-lived.

LX

Whether governing a big country or cooking a little fish, follow Nature's way and no evil tendencies will get control.

This does not mean that the danger of evils can be eliminated entirely, but only that they will cease to harm men.

When ordinary men are unharmed, their leaders are unharmed.

And when nobody harms anybody, perfect harmony prevails.

LXI

To be great, a state must be passively receptive, like the ocean which accepts whatever the rivers bring into it, or like the feminine which always submits to the masculine.

Recall how the female always overcomes the male by means of her passivity.

Passivity is submissiveness.

Thus a great state places itself at the service of a small state before it absorbs the small state.

And a small state must serve the interests of the great state before it can be taken into the great state.

Hence, some submit in order to take, while others submit in order to be taken.

When a great state desires to have more people, and a small state desires to be protected, it is by submission that both obtain what they desire.

LXII

Nature is profoundly worth while.

It is that which is most worth while for good men,

And it is the only real value for bad men.

Flattery may gain favors, and gifts may help one to advance,

But bad men know how to flatter and bribe.

Therefore when leaders are installed in office,

Better than he who artfully gives lavish gifts and glowing tribute,

Is one who, by doing nothing but accepting his natural role as a follower, pays genuine homage.

Why have men always valued Nature?

Was it not because Nature submitted humbly to the task of benefitting the good and the bad alike?

Is not this the reason why it is the most worth while thing in the world?

LXIII

Act disinterestedly—without intending that your action shall change the course of Nature.

Behave indifferently—without trying to impose your own ideas upon the lives of others.

Appreciate natural flavors—without adulterating natural foods with artificial flavors.

Accept the fact that what is small grows big, and what are few become many.

Respond intelligently even to unintelligent treatment.

Take care of what is difficult while it is still easy, and deal with what will become big while it is yet small;

For all difficult things originate in what is easy,

And all big things start from small beginnings.

Therefore the intelligent man, although never troubling himself with big things, still accomplishes the same result (by dealing with them when they are small).

Promising (and refraining from promising) is easy, but fulfilling promises is hard.

He who is careless about things when they are easy will have to face them when they become difficult.

Therefore the intelligent man, although dealing with things which will become difficult, does so by attending to them while they are not difficult.

LXIV

That which remains quiet is easy to handle.

That which has not yet developed is easy to manage.

That which is weak is easy to control.

That which is still small is easy to direct.

Deal with little troubles before they become big.

Attend to little problems before they get out of hand.

For the largest tree was once a sprout,

The tallest tower started with a first brick,

And the longest journey began with a first step.

Just as he who tries to hasten what is natural harms it,

So he who tries to retard what is natural, must fail in his attempt.

Since the intelligent man does not seek to accelerate, he does not make waste,

And since he does not try to restrain, he does not fail.

People are as likely to go wrong in not letting things come to their normal conclusion as they are in not letting them start in their own way.

Be as careful not to interfere with the natural ending of things as with their natural beginning.

The intelligent man has no desire to redirect and no desire for what is hard to get.

He has learned to be unlearned, and has returned to the ways which learned men have forgotten.

He lets each thing develop in its own way, without any attempt to intervene.

LXV

Originally people knew how to follow Nature,

For they did not try to arouse in the people an interest in cunning, but let them remain unspoiled.

The shrewder people are, the harder they are to govern.

Therefore to try to improve government by means of increasing cleverness in the people is to endanger it.

But to improve government by encouraging honesty in the people is beneficial.

To comprehend the significance of these two ways is to have a basis for sound judgment.

To keep this basis for sound judgment always in mind is to be profoundly intelligent.

Profound intelligence is that penetrating and pervading power

To restore all things to their original harmony.

LXVI

Rivers and seas dominate the landscape,

Because, by being good at seeking the lowest places, they fill and occupy and spread over everything.

Likewise the intelligent man is superior to others,

Because he admits that he is inferior,

And he is a leader of others,

Because he is willing to be a follower.

Thus although he is actually superior to others, they do not feel depressed.

And when he leads them, they do not feel that they are being forced to obey.

So all are happy to give him their support.

Since he competes with no one, no one competes with him.

LXVII

Everyone says: "Nature is great, yet Nature is simple."

It is great because it is simple.

If it were not simple, long ago it would have come to little.

Nature sustains itself through three precious principles, which one does well to embrace and follow.

These are gentleness, frugality and humility.

When one is gentle, he has no fear of retaliation.

When one is frugal, he can afford to be generous.

When one is humble, no one challenges his leadership.

But when rudeness replaces gentleness,

And extravagance replaces frugality,

And pride replaces humility,

Then one is doomed.

Since a gentle attack arouses little antagonism,

And a gentle defense provokes little anger,

Nature predisposes to gentleness those most suited for survival.

LXVIII

The best soldier does not attack.

The superior fighter succeeds without violence.

The greatest conqueror wins without a struggle.

The most successful manager leads without dictating.

This is called intelligent nonaggressiveness.

This is called mastery of men.

This is called matching the wisdom of the highest and oldest in Nature.

LXIX

Military maxims say:

"It is easier to defend than to attack."

"It is better to back away a foot than to assault to gain an inch."

This means that the best way to advance is to retreat.

He who bares his flesh will appear to have no need for carrying weapons.

He who does not flourish weapons appears to have nothing to defend.

He who does not prepare to defend himself appears to have no enemies.

No one will attack a person unless he appears to be an enemy,

For to attack one who is not an enemy is to lose a friend.

Therefore, when opposing enemies meet for open battle, he who runs away to hide is the one who wins.

LXX

The things I am saying are very easy to understand and very easy to practice.

Yet no one in the world can comprehend them fully nor practice them perfectly.

The things I am saying did not originate with me but have their source in Nature.

It is because men do not understand this source that they do not understand me.

Since those who understand me are few, they are, for that reason, all the more worthy of emulation.

Therefore the intelligent man presents a poor exterior, yet carries Nature's riches embedded in his core.

LXXI

To know how little one knows is to have genuine knowledge.

Not to know how little one knows is to be deluded.

Only he who knows when he is deluded can free himself from such delusion.

The intelligent man is not deluded, because he knows and accepts his ignorance as ignorance, and thereby has genuine knowledge.

LXXII

Do not be irritated when people do not recognize your importance;

For if you are really important, sooner or later circumstances will force them to recognize it.

Do not treat them contemptuously nor despise them;

For only when you do not despise them will they not despise you.

Although the intelligent man knows his own importance,

He does not require that others recognize it;

And he esteems himself for what he is,

But he does not insist that others esteem him.

He does not seek to be esteemed by others because he recognizes his self-esteem as sufficient.

LXXIII

He whose courage expresses itself as defiance is often put to death.

He whose courage manifests itself as patience to endure insult continues to live.

Of these two kinds of courage, the one is beneficial, the other harmful.

Many people are puzzled as to why, of two courageous men, one is harmed and one benefitted.

But the intelligent man finds no difficulty with this question.

Nature itself has the patience to endure insult, yet always wins in the end.

It does not explain; nevertheless all understand.

It does not command; but all eventually obey.

It does not hurry; yet everything is accomplished.

Nature's web is so wisely woven—wide enough to catch the biggest, fine enough to catch the smallest—that not a single thing escapes.

LXXIV

It is futile to threaten people with death.

If they are not afraid to die, they cannot be frightened by the death-penalty;

And if they are afraid to die, why should we kill them?

Only Nature knows the proper time for a man to die.

To kill is to interrupt Nature's design for dying,

Like a blundering apprentice judging himself to be wiser than his master.

Whenever an apprentice thinks he is smarter than his master, he is very likely to hurt himself.

LXXV

Those who make their living by collecting taxes cause the people to starve; when the people starve, the tax collectors, having no one to tax, starve also.

Those who govern people make them discontented with being controlled; and therefore cause them to be uncontrollable.

Those who are so eager to make a better living that they risk death in doing so are the very ones most likely to die.

Only the self-sufficient person who depends upon and endangers no one else in order to get his living is most sure to live.

LXXVI·

At birth, a man is soft and weak—yet capable of living the whole life ahead of him.

At death, he is hard and tough—yet unable to live for even a minute longer.

All things, whether plants or animals, while living, are soft and weak,

But, when dead, are hard and tough.

Thus hardness and toughness are allied with death,

While softness and weakness are interrelated with life.

This is the reason why the tougher fighters are more likely to be killed,

And the harder trees are more likely to be cut down.

Therefore it is better to be soft and weak than to be hard and tough.

LXXVII

Nature's way is like the bending of a bow:

The top which is high is lowered while the bottom which is low is raised,

And the width which is narrow is widened while the length which is long is shortened.

Nature's way is to take away from those that have too much and give to those that have too little.

Man's way, on the contrary, is to take away from those who have too little in order to give more to those who already have too much.

Which kind of man is able to take away from his own more than enough and give to others who have less than enough?

Only he who embodies Nature's way within himself.

Such a man gives his gift without desiring a reward,

Achieves benefit for others without expecting approbation,

And is generous without calling attention to his generosity.

LXXVIII

Nothing is weaker than water;

Yet, for attacking what is hard and tough,

Nothing surpasses it, nothing equals it.

The principle, that what is weak overcomes what is strong,

And what is yielding conquers what is resistant,

Is known to everyone.

Yet few men utilize it profitably in practice.

But the intelligent man knows that:

He who willingly takes the blame for disgrace to his community is considered a responsible person,

And he who submissively accepts responsibility for the evils in his community naturally will be given enough authority for dealing with them.

These principles, no matter how paradoxical, are sound.

LXXIX

Making agreements and then quarrelling when they are broken is never advisable.

For even when a quarrel is patched up, some animosity will remain.

How can this be considered good?

Therefore the intelligent man continues to carry out his side of a bargain

Even though he does not demand of others that they fulfill their promises

The righteous insist on keeping agreements to the letter,

And the indiscreet foolishly neglect or break their agreements;

But Nature neither keeps nor breaks contracts (because it makes none).

And its ways are good for men.

LXXX

The ideal state is a small intimate community

Where all the necessities of life are present in abundance.

There everyone is satisfied to live and die without looking around for greener pastures.

Even if they have cars or boats, they do not use them for traveling abroad.

Even if they have police and fortifications, these are never put to use.

Business transactions are simple enough to be calculated on one's fingers rather than requiring complicated bookkeeping.

The people are satisfied with their food,

Contented with their clothing,

Comfortable in their dwellings,

And happy with their customs.

Even though neighboring communities are within sight,

And the crowing of the neighbor's cocks and barking of the neighbor's dogs are within hearing,

They grow old and die without ever troubling themselves to go outside of their own communities.

LXXXI

He who is genuine is not artificial;

He who is artificial is not genuine.

He who is intelligent is not quarrelsome;

He who is quarrelsome is not intelligent.

He who is wise is not pretentious;

He who is pretentious is not wise.

Therefore the intelligent man does not struggle to achieve for himself.

The more useful he is to others, the more he will be taken care of by others.

The more he yields to the wishes of others, the more his needs will be cared for by those repeatedly benefitted by his yielding.

Nature's way is to produce good without evil.

The intelligent man's way is to accept and follow Nature rather than to oppose Nature.

COMMENTS BY THE AUTHOR

Lao Tzu

When, where and how the author of the *Tao Teh King* lived have been questions of long and ardent, but largely futile, speculation. The scant historical evidence yields little but doubt, and a few interesting legends. Nevertheless, someone did write or edit the work—if not Lao Tzu, then someone else, either by the same or a different name. And what is important for us today is not who wrote the work but what it says—its profound and penetrating philosophy.

However, for those who are curious, it may be pointed out that the name *Lao* means old, ancient, venerable, and that *Tzu*[1] is a common term of respect, like Sir, Master, or Worthy One. The Chinese, early and late, have venerated the wisdom of their elders. Since the *Tao Teh King* expounds ideals which are exceedingly primitive,[2] and which it attributes to the men of old, one may easily infer that the name of the author[3] means simply "Ancient Thinker," i.e., whoever was the thinker

[1] Or Tzŭ, Tsu, Tse, Tsze, Tz, Ts, Tzyy, Dz. Pronounced explosively, like the "tz" in tzar or the "ts" in nuts.

[2] Both in the sense of primal or primary and of early or ancient.

[3] Which some think was attached to the work by later editors.

of such ancient thoughts. However, others believe that tradition warrants considering Lao Tzu a particular person, identifying him with Lao Tan or Erh Li; but disputes remain as to whether Lao Tzu, Lao Tan and Erh Li were the same or different persons.

Although the date, 570 B.C., has been traditionally accepted as the birth date of Lao Tzu, some recent scholars judge it to be as late as the fourth century.[4] This date may not be of great importance, for Lao Tzu himself "asserts that all of his teachings are actually those of Huang-Ti, the legendary civilizer of China, who is supposed to have ruled the land in 2697 B.C."[5] The Shaping of the philosophy of the *Tao Teh King* is doubtless the work of many minds both before and after Lao Tzu, Lao Tan or Erh Li, regardless of when he, or they, lived. The ideals are extremely ancient; yet the claim that its later forms reflect editing by persons wishing to refute Confucius is not without merit. Although the authorship of the *Tao Teh King* is still controversial, the established practice of crediting it to Lao Tzu will be followed.

[4] See Hu Shih, "A Criticism of Some Recent Methods Used in Dating Lao Tzu," *The Harvard Journal of Asiatic Studies,* Vol. II, Dec., 1937, pp. 373-397; Homer H. Dubs, "The Date and Circumstances of the Philosopher Lao-dz," *Journal of the American Oriental Society,* Vol. LXI, Dec., 1941, pp. 215-221; Derk Bodde, "The New Identification of Lao Tzŭ," *Ibid.,* Vol. LXII, March, 1942, pp. 8-13; Homer H. Dubs, "The Identification of Lao Dz," *Ibid.,* Vol. LXII, Dec., 1942, pp. 300-304; Derk Bodde, "Further Remarks on the Identification of Lao Tzŭ," *Ibid.,* Vol. LXIV, March, 1944, pp. 24-27; Fung Yu-lan, *The History of Chinese Philosophy,* Vol. I, Ch. VIII; Fung Yu-lan, *A Short History of Chinese Philosophy,* p. 93.

[5] Charles F. Horne, *Sacred Books and Early Literature of the East,* Vol. XII, p. 2. Parke, Austin and Lipscomb, Inc., N.Y. and London, 1895, 1917.

Tao Teh King

King (*Ching, Jing*) means book.[6] A *King* consists of a collection of written (i.e., painted or carved) Chinese characters. Early *King* were composed by painting a series of symbols down one bamboo stalk, then another and another, and then tying the stalks together to form a roll. The *Tao Teh King* is a book about *Tao* and *Teh* which, as we shall see, are not two different things but two aspects of one and the same thing. We shall inquire first into the nature of *Tao*[7] and then into the nature of *Teh*.[8]

Tao

Tao—the most basic concept in Chinese philosophy—has been variously translated into English, but no translation is quite adequate. Many of the translations, as will be shown in the following, miss the mark widely. This concept, indigenous to Chinese culture, needs to be understood in terms of its original setting. Yet, also, being at once simple and yet very profound, it embodies certain ideas which are common to all mankind. When one first encounters a foreign word with unfamiliar conceptual overtones, he immediately looks for analogues in his own culture. Nothing quite fits. Hence it suffers by comparison. Since Tao is a concept of ultimate reality, "prior to all beginnings and endings, which, unmoved and unmanifest, itself neither begins nor ends, all-pervasive

---

[6] Relative to the *Tao Teh King,* King is occasionally translated as treatise, canon, and classic.

[7] Pronounced "dao" or "dow" with an explosive "d."

[8] Or Têh, Te, Tê, De, Der.

and inexhaustible, perpetual source of everything else" (25),[9] each translater looks for that in his own culture which best expresses his idea of ultimate reality. Western theists (e.g., Hebrew, Christian, Moslem) call this Jahweh, God, or Allah, while Hindus call it Brahman. Followers of Plato try to identify it with the "Idea of the Good," of the Stoics with "Logos," of Spinoza with "Nature"; Hegelians and other absolute idealists with "The Absolute," Bergsonians with "Elan Vital," Emersonians with "The Oversoul," Freudians with "Cosmic Libido," and materialists, if they bother to be interested, with "Matter," "Energy," or "Mattergy." Tao has been translated as "Principle" or "Creative Principle," as "Truth," not abstract truth but as "Concrete Truth," and as "divine intelligence" of the universe (Lin Yutang, p. 14).[10]

But none of these is adequate because each entails, or is likely to entail in the minds of most readers, certain additional characteristics or emphases not intended by the original. One of the better translations is "Way" (with unsatisfactory variations, "Path," "Method"), partly because what this term connotes is sufficiently simple, unpretentious, ambiguous, and at the same time universal and, what is best of all, immediately or intuitively apprehendable by all. Yet this term suffers from the suggestion that it, like "Path" or "Road," is something to walk upon or an external and preexistent guide for one's steps. The term "Mana," commonly employed by anthropologists to denote invisible causes of visible effects, although usually overlooked by interpreters, is, because of its primitive char-

[9] Numerals in parentheses immediately after quotations indicate the number of the section (or "chapter") in the text.

[10] Numerals after the name of an author quoted refer to page numbers of books listed in the Bibliography.

acter, no less closely related to the concept of Tao than most other common analogies.

After surveying all the traditional usages and other suggested possibilities, the writer has chosen the previously-used term "Nature" or, alternatively, "Existence" as the most nearly adequate term in English. Tao is "Nature" with a capital "N." "In Nature, all natures originate. . . . Yet, no matter how many natures come into being, they can never exhaust Nature. To look for an external source of Nature is foolish, for Nature is the source of all else." (4) "Ultimate reality is all-pervasive; it is immanent everywhere. All other things owe their existence to it and draw their sustenance from it." (34) "Nature contains nothing but natures; and these natures are nothing over and above Nature." (4)

Some interpreters jump to the conclusion that, since Nature is all-pervasive and there is nothing over and above or before or after Nature, Nature must be one. But this is a mistake. Nature is both one and many, though why and in what ways may be forever beyond our comprehension. It is obvious, however, that things appear in Nature as opposites, and that the principle of opposition is universal. "Consider how Nature operates. Some things precede while others follow. Some things blow one way while some blow another. Some things are strong while others are weak. Some things are going up while others are going down." (29) "Nature's way is a joint process of initiation and completion, sowing and reaping, producing and consuming." (10) Not only are opposites all-pervasive, (6) but, in each pair of dynamic opposites, it may be noted that one initiates and the other completes, the one arouses and the other satisfies, the one starts and the other finishes, the one activates and the other perfects, the one is aggressive, the other submissive, the one active, the other passive, the one positive, the other its negative. (7) Chinese thought, long before Lao Tzu, had named and symbolized these two opposing tendencies of initiating and completing as *Yang* and *Yin*. Yang (represented by an unbroken line —) exists wherever there is initiation, activation, growth, development. Yin (represented by a broken line — —) exists wherever there is completion, submission, decline, perfection.[11]

Nature changes, yet always remains the same. Nature operates cyclically: sunrise is followed by sunset, day by night, spring by fall, birth by death. Nature "involves initiation of growth, initiation of growth involves completion of growth, and completion of growth involves returning to that whence it came." (25) But also night is followed by day, fall by spring, death by birth. "Nature alternates dynamically. When it completes what it is doing, then it starts all over again. All that is springs from such alternation." (40) "Nature first begets one thing. Then one thing begets another. The two produce a third. In this way, all things are begotten. Why? Because all things are impregnated by the two alternating tendencies, the tendency toward completion, and the tendency toward initiation, which, acting together, complement each other." (42) "Nature treats opposites impartially, dealing with each of every pair of opposites with the same indifference.

---

[11] The *Yi King (I Ching)* or *Book of Changes* elaborates and interprets sixty-four hexigrams composed of the various permutations of combinations of six lines, broken and unbroken. How much these influenced Lao Tzu is uncertain, but the general concept of opposites, symbolized by Yang and Yin, is inherent in his conception of Tao.

No matter how deeply natures are torn by opposition, Nature itself remains unchanged." (5)

Just as Nature changes and yet remains the same, so Nature acts without acting or without exerting itself. Nature's action is spontaneous. It cannot be imposed upon from the outside, for there is nothing prior to, other than, or outside of, Nature to influence it. It can neither be persuaded nor dissuaded. (56) "No one else can tell it what to do." (32) So Nature acts naturally, or in accordance with its own nature, for there is nothing other than it to activate it. And there is nothing other than Nature for Nature to act upon. Hence all its action is self-action. Now when something does not influence or produce effects upon other things, it appears uninfluential or ineffective. Or when one thing does not act upon anything else, its not acting may be thought of as inaction. Since there is nothing outside Nature for it to act upon, its internal self-action appears, externally, like inaction. In this sense, "Nature never acts, yet it activates everything." (37) "All aiming is Nature's aiming, and is Nature's way of being itself." (25) "Whoever acts naturally is Nature itself acting." (23) Hence Nature accepts all action as its own. "Whatever is produced, Nature accepts it for what it is. However it behaves, Nature lets it follow its own way." (51) "Nature produces things, and Nature's instincts guide them. Although different in kind, each thing has its own self-sufficient instinct to guide it. Nothing can fail to emulate Nature and instinct by embodying them within its own life. Such emulation is not demanded, but occurs of its own accord." (*Ibid.*) "Having created them and nurtured them, it does not demand title to them. Even though it has provided for all, it refuses to dominate over a single one. Since it asks nothing in return for its services, it may appear of little worth. But all things return home to it again, even though they do not know that they are being called home." (34)

Is Tao, then, the same as God—the God of Christians and Jews and Muslims? It is like God, or God is like it, in being the uncreated source, the uncaused cause, of all else, in being self-acting, in serving as a guide for men to emulate, and in calling men home whether they know it or not. But God is a person, or at least personal, whereas Tao is impersonal. Theists usually oppose God to the world, whereas Tao is the world itself; or they oppose two worlds, this world to the next world, whereas Tao is the only world; or they oppose the natural to the supernatural, whereas there is nothing supernatural in Tao and nothing superior to Tao. God loves and cares for his creatures. Tao accepts and nurtures its creatures, but does so without anxiety, without wanting its creatures to do otherwise than they will do, and hence is indifferent in the sense that it has no desire to interfere with whatever they do or to prevent whatever happens to befall them. Although it is true that "Nature procreates all things and then devotes itself to caring for them," (10) it cares for them as soil cares for a plant or as a cow cares for its calf. The soil awaits for the seed to use its nourishment if it wishes, but does not rush about excitedly urging: "Seed grow in me." The cow devotes itself to producing milk for its calf, but does not chase about after its calf crying: "Come and drink." Each freely gives what it has to give, but it does not seek to impose its gift upon those who may receive it. Thus Tao both cares and does not care. It cares enough to "originate and suckle, rear and develop, protect and provide for, and guide and perfect all things." (51) Yet it has no anxiety about their welfare, for each will come naturally to its own end (death) anyway, sooner or later. To care, to be anxious, is to be distrustful of Nature's way; and the depth of our love or the violence of our hatred or the strength of our fear or the bitterness of our disappointment all are measures of our distrust of Tao. But Tao has no distrust; hence Tao cannot care.

In contrast to those concerned with "doing God's will," who thus must fear evil consequences of displeasing God, followers of Lao Tzu find that impersonal Tao has no will, at least nothing that can choose, decide, favor, or change its course. Tao has no will to impose itself upon any one of its creatures in any way; "however it behaves, Nature lets it follow its own way." (51) Tao has no forethought, no pre-knowledge, no after-thought, no memory, no fears, and no regrets. "Nature is already as good as it can be," (29) so for Nature to think about itself, worry about itself, or want itself to be different, would all be useless.

Many theists believe in personal immortality. But how can one who observes Nature completing and perfecting each thing, being born, growing to maturity, declining, and dying, living its life to the full, expect or desire anything further? Are those dissatisfied with what Nature has provided for them in this life likely to be any more satisfied if Nature should happen to provide them with another life? He who trusts Nature's way as best for him can feel assured that the fulfillment of the life which Nature has provided for him is all he needs and all he should desire. He may, if he wishes, appreciate the fact that his own nature realizing itself is Nature's way of realizing itself through him, and that thus he is a genuine expression of an everlasting process; but whether he does or does not so appreciate makes no difference to Nature.

Persons, although genuinely different from each other, have no existence separate from Nature. And prayer is useless, for Nature cannot be influenced. (56)

Now if it be objected that some theists are pantheists, and that God is really impersonal, then evaluation of the similarities between Tao and God will be different. But examination of the many varieties of pantheism will not be attempted here. Lin Yutang (p. 14) speaks of Tao as the "divine intelligence" of the universe. But Tao is not an intelligence of the universe, but the universe itself acting intelligently. Tao is not merely a force pervading existence, but is existence itself existing in the way it exists.

If Tao is so unlike God, a Western conception, is Tao like Brahman (of Advaita Vedanta), another oriental conception? Again there are similarities. Both are thought of as a changeless ultimate source of all. Both are alike in being impersonal, impartial, incapable of being influenced, and ever available for all to use, though indifferent as to whether they are used or not. They are also alike in being that to which all things come home at last (32, 34), and in existing within persons, Tao as tao, and Brahman as atman or jiva. But there are differences also. Brahman is an eternal, i.e., timeless, unity whose real nature is to remain unstirred. Tao, on the other hand, is essentially temporal, omni-temporal or everlasting, to be sure, but always acting in temporal cycles with beginnings and endings. "Deep in its depths are activating forces. No matter how unplumbable the depths, these forces unfailingly sustain the world as it appears to us." (21) Brahman contains no forces within it, for it is a pure unity freed from all distinction, differentiation, plurality. It is, even, beyond the distinction between unity and plurality. All distinction, all plurality, all individuality, and all time are unreal, illusory, or *maya.* It is true that there are reincarnations and "Days and Nights of Brahman," but these too are waves of illusion, which may be extinguished by yogic practices, withdrawal from life, devotion to subjectivity. Brahman is the epitome of spirituality. Tao is not spiritual but natural. Tao is not a bare unity, but a unity in plurality, in which the plurality, the many taos, are genuinely real. In Tao, change is real, and Tao is ever-changing, and the way of change, or reversal of beginning (yang) and ending (yin), is real. "Nature is ultimate, the principle of initiating is ultimate, the principle of perfecting is ultimate. And the intelligent person is ultimate." (25) But in Brahman, all illusory individuality, or personality, disappears.

Although "Nature is already as good as it can be," it is not the same as Plato's "Idea of the Good." "The Good" is an ideal, an ought, a goal. Tao is an actuality, an *is,* an on-going self-contained process. Plato makes form prior to matter, the universal prior to particulars, and the changeless prior to change. The *Tao Teh King* suggests no need for making one of these prior to the other. Tao, "the formless source of all forms," (14) is not merely a source, but also the flow, and the terminus of all things; and both form and matter, universal and particular, changelessness and change, have their being in Tao. Plato's Idea of the Good stands at the pinnacle of a hierarchy of universals prior to particulars. But the *Tao Teh King* deplores both ideals of hierarchy (superiority and inferiority) (3) and of abstraction. (1, 2)

Tao is profoundly similar to the Stoic "Logos." And in Stoicism is to be found the closest parallel to Taoism in Western culture. However, unfortunately, Stoicism is not widely known, despite the prominent place given to it in histories of

philosophy. Following Heraclitus, Stoics see God or Nature as
" 'day and night, winter and summer, war and peace, satiety
and hunger; but he takes various shapes, just as fire, when it is
mingled with different incenses, is named according to the
savour of each.' These aphorisms are hard to understand.
Presumably they mean that there is a 'One' constituted by
'opposites,' and that the 'opposites' are disclosed by self-
division of the 'One.' What, then, was the 'One'? 'This order,
which is the same in all things, no one of gods or men has
made; but ever was, is now, and ever shall be an ever-living
Fire, fixed measures of it kindling and fixed measures of it
going out.' "[12] " 'Eternal return' lurks in the system of the
universe inseparable from its maintenance. A crisis must occur
when the Many revert to the primogenous Activity and, when
'tone' has been reestablished, the entire process will repeat itself."[13] The Stoic universe is pantheistic; all of its parts are in
harmony. Man's nature reflects the nature of the cosmos, and
man's freedom consists in conformity with nature or in his
personal logos being a willing expression of the cosmic Logos.
The way to happiness is by "acceptance of the universe and of
our place in it."[14] Yet Stoicism appears more rationalistic,
more theistic,[15] more ascetic, and more sophisticated[16] than

[12] R. M. Wenley, *Stoicism,* pp. 81-82. Longmans, Green and Co.,
N.Y., 1924, 1927.

[13] *Ibid.,* p. 84.

[14] W. T. Jones, *A History of Western Philosophy,* Vol. I, p. 271.
Harcourt, Brace and Co., N.Y., 1952.

[15] Its pantheistic God cares, has prevision and will.

[16] I.e., Stoicism is more conscious of opposing views against which
it had to compete and which continue to constitute the setting in
which it is commonly understood. However, some think that the
greater sophistication of later Taoists, such as Chuang Tzu, exhibited

Taoism. Although the fire analogy of the Stoics, borrowed from Heraclitus, is a naturalistic symbol, the naturalism of the *Tao Teh King* needs no analogies, for to interpret any one thing in terms of another does violence to it. Stoics appear to emphasize the place of man in the scheme of things; in Taoism, however, since all things are equally natural, one thing is no more important than another. Lao Tzu needs no universal conflagration to restore things to their original status in Tao; for each things makes its own return in its own way. When the Stoic God is pictured as Zeus "seated at the outermost circle of the world,"[17] it is poles apart from Tao, which is always within the process. However, the difference between the philosophies of the Stoics and of the *Tao Teh King* may be thought of as differences in degree rather than in kind.

If Neo-Platonists were to suggest that Tao is identical with Plotinus' "One," they would be mistaken, for although there is only one Tao, Tao is not merely one. Plotinus claimed that the One is unrelated to the many and that degrees of plurality constitute degrees of unreality. Tao, on the other hand, is both one and many, and each of the many particular taos may be completely real. None of the many taos is external to Tao, and each is as real as Tao to the extent that it acts in accordance with this own nature as Tao does. The Greek law of excluded-middle did not divide Chinese opposites—neither Tao from taos nor Yang from Yin. And, although apparently Plotinus was not wholly consistent, in holding that the One is not

---

in replying to Confucians and School of Names, is already implicit in the *Tao Teh King*. (See Fung Yu-lan, *A Short History of Chinese Philosophy,* pp. 93-94.)

[17] Frank Thilly, *A History of Philosophy,* p. 135. Henry Holt and Co., N.Y., 1914, 1951.

related to the many even though the many are related to the One, Lao Tzu felt no need for such an unnatural and illogical arrangement. Although Tao remains while each tao comes and goes, each tao is as natural, as real, and as ultimate in its own way as Tao is in its way. Plotinus' One is changeless, whereas Tao is always involved in change; Plotinus' One is logically perfect, whereas reversal is the movement whereby Tao perfects itself temporally and "what is most complete is still incomplete; yet it is as complete as it can be" (45); Plotinus' many are opposed to the One, but Tao contains all opposition within it; whereas Plotinus appears to subordinate nature to logic, the concept of Tao subordinates logic to Nature.[18]

Is Tao like Spinoza's pantheistic "Nature"? No, for Spinoza's Nature, a fixed, perfect, deductive, passionless system, is potentially completely knowable, whereas in Tao some things are as naturally passionate as others are naturally impassionate, and knowledge, where it exists, more probably will lead one astray than aright. For Spinoza, ultimate reality reveals itself most clearly in geometrical relationships conceived as universal and necessary, whereas for Lao Tzu ultimate reality most fully exists in whatever acts most wholly in accordance with its own individual nature. Spinoza idealizes the seeking of knowledge, for his Nature is perfectly knowable potentially. But Lao Tzu sees Tao as essentially unknowable (1) and knowledge, which involves an attempted external reconstruc-

[18] Although it may be true that in later Chinese thought "The concept of Tao is a formal one and not a positive one" (Fung Yu-lan, *A Short History of Chinese Philosophy*, p. 96. The Macmillan Co., N.Y., 1948,) it is a mistake to read this formalism back into the original thoughts.

tion of what is essentially internal, may be either useless or misleading; it is useless because the natures known are already self-sufficient beings and thus cannot be aided by external interference, and it is misleading to the extent that it tempts us to direct, and thus interfere with, the course of Nature. The true way to know is to be; all other knowledge is artificial.

Is Tao "Truth"? (See Cheng Lin, *The Works of Lao Tzyy: Truth and Nature*.) If "Truth" means Existence, i.e., that which makes our beliefs true, rather than the true beliefs, i.e., beliefs about Existence, then yes. But this meaning of the term "Truth," although not unknown in Western thought, is not the most usual one and hence may easily mislead readers. The question of truth, at least in its modern Western senses, is not raised in the *Tao Teh King* except in its opening section where it warns against trying "to express the inexpressible" and making "distinctions which are unreal." "He who desires to know Nature as it is in itself will not try to express it in words." (1)

How is Tao like "The Absolute" of Hegel and other Absolute Idealists? Both are concrete, both embody opposites, both appear paradoxical. Everything within Tao is opposed to something else, and everything has opposition within itself, at least its beginning and its ending (See 2, 4, 5, 6, 7, 11, 36, 40, 41); even Tao is, in a sense, opposed to taos. Yang and yin function as thesis and antithesis. But the Absolute of the Idealists is idealistic whereas Tao or Nature is naturalistic. The "reversal" which is the "movement of Tao" is, like sunrise and sunset, arousing and subsiding, birth and death, a natural cycle, whereas the dialectic of The Absolute is primarily a logical movement.

"Mana," the term widely employed by anthropologists as a

common name for "nature powers," should not be overlooked when seeking analogies. Tao and mana are alike in many ways. Both are primitive concepts, both function primarily as the invisible cause of visible effects, both are highly ambiguous and difficult, if not impossible, to understand fully. Both are prior in nature to any distinction between personal and impersonal, rational and irrational, one and many, spirit and matter, good and evil. However, there are differences, though such differences are difficult to discuss since there are so many varieties of mana. Later Taoistic religious practices reincorporated animistic magical practices. Tao is a more comprehensive concept, since mana is usually thought of as a spirit or force embodied, temporarily or permanently, in nature and natural objects, whereas Tao is Nature or nature's own force functioning not merely in, but as, nature and natural objects. Mana may be whimsical, slippery, uncertain, and may work harm as well as good, or some kinds of mana always harm and some forms always good. Consequently, animists tend to be constantly alert to the need for influencing, capturing or warding off, other mana and of protecting and increasing one's own mana. But for Lao Tzu, "Nature's way is to produce good without evil." (81) Hence calmness, gentleness, and refusal to try to influence other natures replace the need for alertness as an ideal. The animist resorts to magic; the naturalist let's nature take her course.

Teh

Teh is the power of Nature to be natural or of anything to follow its own nature. Tao and Teh are not two different things. Yet they are distinguishable. If it is natural for Tao to act naturally, and if Teh is the ability of Tao to act naturally, what is the difference between them? Teh is the ability of Tao to be itself. Now such a distinction would never have arisen were it not for the fact that some beings do not act in accordance with their own natures. Some men try to modify their nature by seeking to prolong or shorten, to hasten or retard, to magnify or minimize their natural activities. But "those too eager for activity soon become fatigued. When things exhaust their vigor, they age quickly. Such impatience is against Nature. What is against Nature dies young." (55) Also, some men try to impose their wishes, hence their natures, upon others, thus forcing these others to act unnaturally or not in accordance with their own natures. And some men are imposed upon by others and thus act unnaturally or in accordance with a nature which is not their own. "Whoever acts unnaturally will come to an unnatural finish." (30) Now, since it is obvious that some things do not follow their own natures and some things do, those who do must have the ability to do so, and this ability is Teh.

Teh is the power of a thing to be itself, to live its own life, to act its own actions. "It is by self-activity that all things fulfil themselves. . . . If self-activity did not govern, then disruption would set in." (39) "For a thing cannot function properly when its own nature has been disrupted." (48) "Each thing which grows and develops to the fullness of its own nature completes its course by declining in a manner inherently determined by its own nature. Completing its life is as inevitable as that each thing shall have its own goal." (16) "The way to success is this: having achieved your goal, be satisfied not to go further. For this is the way Nature operates." (9) "To be in accord with Nature is to be achieving the goal of life. But to seek excitement is to invite calamity." (55)

Teh is inner activity, but not inactivity, as is often said. Teh is the power to be simple, i.e., simply oneself, without involving oneself unnecessarily in the affairs of others. It is the ability to "accept what is as it is." (2) "If you see what is small as it sees itself, and accept what is weak for what strength it has, and use what is dim for the light it gives, then all will go well." (52) "What, then, must we do in order to achieve contentment? Let each thing act according to its own nature, and it will eventually come to rest in its own way." (15) "Therefore the intelligent man expresses his beneficence to other men by accepting each man's own way as best for himself. And he performs the same service for all other beings, for he willingly recognizes that, by following its own nature, each thing does the best that can be done for it." (27) "There is no greater evil than desiring to change others. There is no greater misfortune than desiring to change oneself. . . . Only he who is satisfied with whatever satisfactions his own nature provides for him is truly satisfied." (46)

Teh is intelligence, for intelligence is ability to achieve one's genuine goals. He who misses the mark, falls short, fails, is unintelligent. "Intelligence consists in acting according to Nature." (21, 81) "The truth is that whatever is natural is good." (50) "By acting naturally, one reaps Nature's rewards. So by acting intelligently, one achieves intelligent goals. Whereas by acting unintelligently, one comes to an unintelligent end." (23) "The intelligent man adheres to the genuine and discards the superficial." (38) Intelligence is also adaptability. "Wise behavior adapts itself appropriately to the particular circumstances." (8) "The best way to conduct oneself may be observed in the behavior of water" (*Ibid.*), because it is "good at seeking the lowest places." (66) It accepts the unoccupied spaces, adapts itself to the contours of other things without disturbing them, moves quietly and gently along its course. Since it "competes with no one, no one competes with it." (*Ibid.*) "Nature predisposes to gentleness those most suited for survival." (67) Furthermore, intelligence is ability to act prudently. "Take care of what is difficult while it is still easy, and deal with what will become big while it is yet small." (63) Why? Because these "are the easiest ways." (8)

Teh has been translated as "power" (Waley) and power it is. But it is more than mere power. It is intelligent power. It is not "magic power" (Duyvendak, p. 8; Blakney, pp. 38-39), for it is not power to interfere with, influence, or change the course of nature (work miracles). Rather it is "virtue" (Carus, Giles, Duyvendak) in the original Latin meaning of the term. Virtue is virility or strength of anything which is able to fulfil its functions. Teh is the "vitality" (Goddard) of things to live their own lives.

Teh is the ability to keep within limits. "When the intelligent man hears about Nature's alternating way, he seeks to embody it within himself." (41) "We profit equally by the positive and negative ingredients in each situation." (11) "If Nature's way is a joint process of initiating and completing, sowing and reaping, producing and consuming, can you rightly demand that you deserve always to play the role of consumer?" (10) "Nature's way is to take away from those that have too much and give to those that have too little." (77) "Going to extremes is never best." (9) "The intelligent man avoids both extremes, shunning excess in one way as well as in the other." (29) "Those who fully comprehend the true nature of existence do not try to push things to excess. And because they do not try to push things to excess, they are able to satisfy their needs repeatedly without exhausting themselves." (15) "He who is wise lets well enough alone." (30)

Teh is the ability to remain self-sufficient even as Nature is self-sufficient. "The inner self is our true self; so in order to realize our true self, we must be willing to live without being dependent upon the opinion of others. . . . Pride and shame cause us much fearful anxiety. . . . Pride attaches undue importance to the superiority of one's status in the eyes of others. And shame is fear of humiliation . . . in the estimation of others. When one sets his heart on being highly esteemed, and achieves such rating, then he is automatically involved in fear of losing his status. The protection of his status appears to be his most important need. And humiliation seems the worst of all evils. . . . He who wisely devotes himself to being self-sufficient, and therefore does not depend for his happiness upon external ratings by others, is the one best able to set an example for, and to teach and govern, others." (13) "The intelligent man presents a poor exterior, yet carries Nature's richness embedded in his core." (70) "Only the self-sufficient person who depends upon and endangers no one else in order to get his living is most sure to live." (75) "He who receives his happiness from others may be rich, but he whose contentment is self-willed has inexhaustible wealth." (33) He is "as unconcerned as the rolling ocean, without a care to bother him." (20)

Teh is also the ability to refrain from meddling in the lives of others. "There is no greater vice than desiring to change things." (46) "Whoever gives up his desire to improve upon Nature will find Nature satisfying all his needs." (22) "He lets each thing develop in its own way, without any attempt to intervene" (64), and "without trying to impose (his) own ideas upon the lives of others." (63) "Being intelligent, he knows that each has a nature which is able to take care of itself." (16) "Whenever someone sets out to remold the world, experience teaches that he is bound to fail." (29) "If one remains silent and keeps to himself, he will not fail to fulfil his life; but if he gives advice and meddles in other's affairs, he invites trouble." (52) "When I attend to my own business, other people are able to attend to theirs." (57)

Finally, Teh is ability to achieve without effort. "The intelligent man has no desire . . . for what is hard to get." (64) "Nature's way is simple and easy, but (unintelligent) men prefer the intricate and artificial." (53) Nature "does not hurry; yet everything is accomplished." (73) "That which is most yielding eventually overcomes what is most resistant." (43) "The intelligent man does not struggle to achieve for himself. The more useful he is to others, the more he will be taken care of by others. The more he yields to the wishes of others, the more his needs will be cared for by those repeatedly benefitted by his yielding." (81) "By not competing with others, he achieves without opposition." (22) He does not strive to keep things separated or force them together, for "things which go together naturally do not have to be tied; for they will not separate even without bonds." (27) If he has to deal "with things which will become difficult, (he) does so by attending to them while they are not difficult." (63) "Without going out-of-doors, one can know all he needs to know. . . . Without going beyond his own nature, he can achieve ultimate wisdom. Therefore the intelligent man knows all he needs to know without going away, and sees all he needs to see without looking elsewhere, and does all he needs to do without undue exertion." (47)

The whole doctrine of the *Tao Teh King* is summarized within the text itself, in two different ways. The first: "Everyone says: 'Nature is great, yet Nature is simple.' It is great because it is simple. . . . Nature sustains itself through three precious principles, which one does well to embrace and follow. These are gentleness, frugality and humility. (These have come to be called the "three jewels" or gems of wisdom of Taoism.) When one is gentle, he has no fear of retaliation. When one is frugal, he can afford to be generous. When one is humble, no one challenges his leadership." (67) The second: "Simply be yourself. Act naturally. Refrain from self-assertiveness. Avoid covetousness." (19)

Various Topics

If one seeks answers to more specialized questions concerning the nature of knowledge, language, argumentation, law, friendship, gifts, education, esteem, he can find suggestions in this very short work.

Knowledge is secondary to being. Since Nature is already as good as it can be, and cannot be improved upon, the purpose of knowledge is not to understand so that one can control Nature but so that one can accept Nature. "The intelligent man accepts what is as it is. In seeking to grasp what is, he does not devote himself to the making of distinctions which are then mistaken to be separate existences." (2) "When knowledge becomes highly abstract, men are deceived by mistaking abstractions for realities." (18) "While day by day the over-zealous student stores up facts for future use, he who has learned to trust nature finds need for ever fewer external directions. He will discard formula after formula, until he reaches the conclusion: Let Nature take its course." (48) "To know how little one knows is to have genuine knowledge. Not to know how little one knows is to be deluded. Only he who knows when he is deluded can free himself from such delusion. The intelligent man is not deluded, because he knows and accepts his ignorance as ignorance, and thereby has genuine knowledge." (71) "He has learned to be unlearned, and has returned to the ways which learned men have forgotten." (64) He admires the wisdom of the ancients, for "in primitive times, intelligent men had an intuitively penetrating grasp of reality which could not be stated in words." (15)

Language, too, is an area of dangerous pitfalls. "No name can fully express what it represents. . . . If Nature is inexpressible, he who desires to know Nature as it is in itself will not try to express it in words. To try to express the inexpressible leads one to make distinctions which are unreal." (1) "Once one begins to differentiate between one thing and another, how will he know where to stop? To know when to stop making distinctions is to be free from error." (32) "Nothing is gained by representing what fully exists by a description—another lesser, diluted kind of existence." (2) "If we ignore intricate learning and knowledge of petty distinctions, we shall be many times better off." (19) "If we stop fussing about grammatical trivialities, we will get along much better. The difference between 'Yes' and 'Ya' is insignificant as compared with a genuine distinction like 'Good' and 'Bad.' Yet some people are as fearful of making a grammatical mistake as of committing a vital error." (20)

Argumentation, which arises when people take opposing views, finds its principles of solution in Nature's example.

"Each one of many kinds of opposites acts as if it could get along without its other. But Nature treats opposites impartially, dealing with each of every pair of opposites with the same indifference. . . . In conflicts between opposites, the more one attacks his seeming opponent (upon which he really depends for his completion), the more he defeats himself (and thereby demonstrates that only Nature, and not any opposite abstracted from existence, is self-sufficient). So, likewise, no matter how much debaters argue, their argument proves nothing. Things are what they are, regardless of how much we disagree about them." (5) "The intelligent man, when an issue arises, stands off and observes both contentions. Since he does not take sides, he never loses a battle." (7)

Law is of two types. The one: laws of Nature, or natural law, which do not need to be known in order to be followed and which, when violated, bring their own punishment spontaneously. The other: laws which are artificial, or man-made, and which have to be enforced with effort. "Whenever a regulation is imposed from above, it is not willingly obeyed. Then effort is used to enforce it. . . . But where law is enforced, spontaneous and sincere loyalty declines, and disintegration of the harmonious society sets in. Thus valuing law as an end in itself results in minimizing fidelity to Nature itself. Knowledge of law appears at once as a flowering of Nature's way and as the source of error." (38) "Making agreements and then quarrelling when they are broken is never advisable. For even when a quarrel is patched up, some animosity will remain. . . . Therefore the intelligent man continues to carry out his side of the bargain even though he does not demand of others that they fulfil their promises. The righteous insist on keeping agreements to the letter, and the indiscreet foolishly neglect or break their agreements; but Nature neither keeps nor breaks contracts (because it makes none)." (79)

Friendship "should be based upon sympathy and good will." (8) But "the intelligent man is not willful. He accepts what others will for themselves as his will for them. Those who appear good, he accepts, and those who appear bad, he accepts; for Nature accepts both." (49) He "expresses his beneficence to other men by accepting each man's own way as best for himself. And he performs the same service for all other beings, for he willingly recognizes that, by following its own nature, each thing does the best that can be done for it." (27)

Gifts are natural also but there are intelligent and unintelligent ways of giving. "The generous giver gives because he wants to give. The dutiful giver gives because he wants to receive." (38) "Nature's way is to take away from those who have too much to give to those who have too little. Man's way, on the contrary, is to take away from those who have too little in order to give to those who already have too much." (77) The intelligent man "gives his gift without desiring a reward, achieves benefit for others without expecting approbation, and is generous without calling attention to this generosity." (*Ibid.*) Giving away things which you do not need is wise, for "the more you have, the more you have to lose. The more you value things, the less you value your self." (44) "The generous trader needs no scales." (27)

Educational philosophy should take its cues from Nature. "Nature produces things, and Nature's instincts guide them. . . . Nothing can fail to emulate Nature and instinct by embodying them within its own life. Such emulation is not demanded, but occurs of its own accord." (51) "Things which act naturally do not need to be told how to act. The wind and rain begin without being ordered, and quit without being commanded. This is the way with all natural beginnings and endings. If Nature does not have to instruct the wind and rain (and people), how much less should man try to direct them?" (23) "He who has learned to trust Nature finds need for ever fewer external directions." (48) "In teaching, he teaches, not by describing and pointing out differences, but by example." (2) Nature "provides a pattern to follow, without requiring anyone to follow it." (10) "The intelligent person is at one with Nature, and so serves as a model for others." (22) "Those who do not trust Nature as a model cannot be trusted as guides." (23) "Guiding by example rather than by words or commands is most successful." (43) Nature provides a "two-pronged lesson: Bad men can learn from the good man's success. Good men can learn from the bad man's failures. Whoever despises such teachers, whether good or bad, or fails to appreciate such lessons, even though he may be a 'walking encyclopaedia,' is really a misguided fool." (27)

"Esteem by others or self-esteem, which is better? . . . The more you depend upon others for esteem, the less you are self-sufficient." (44) "The esteemed must depend upon others for their esteem, whereas the unesteemed are self-sufficient. . . . For, must not the unesteemed be the basis for the esteemed? Therefore the unesteemed is the ultimate in esteem." (39) "The intelligent man is superior to others, because he admits that he is inferior, and he is a leader of others, because he is willing to be a follower. Thus although he is actually superior to others, they do not feel depressed." (66) "By not boasting of what he will do, he succeeds in doing more than he promises. By not gloating over his success, his achievements are acclaimed by others." (22) "When one is humble, no one challenges his leadership. But when pride . . . replaces humility, then one is doomed." (67) "Do not be irritated when people do not recognize your importance; for if you are really important, sooner or later circumstances will force them to recognize it. Do not treat them contemptuously nor despise them; for only when you do not despise them will they not despise you. Although the intelligent man knows his own importance, he does not require that others recognize it; and he esteems himself for what he is, but does not insist that others esteem him. He does not seek to be esteemed by others because he recognizes his self-esteem as sufficient." (72)

Government

The political and social philosophy of the *Tao Teh King* is anarchistic. Although Lao Tzu was not as anti-social as some critics claim (criticism partly justified of Taoism in general because Yang Chu, another early Taoist, made the startling and seemingly rash statement that he would not pluck out a single hair even though it would profit the whole world), he did idealize rural simplicity in opposition to urban complexity. When people "congregate in artistically engineered cities, and neglect their farms, their food supply is cut off." (53) "The ideal state is a small intimate community where all the necessities of life are present in abundance. There everyone is satisfied to live and die without looking around for greener pastures. . . . Even though neighboring communities are within sight, . . . they grow old and die without ever troubling themselves to go outside of their own communities." (80) There would be no governors or tax collectors, for "those who make their living by collecting taxes cause the people to starve;

when the people starve, the tax collectors, having no one to
tax, starve also. Those who govern people make them discontented with being controlled therefore cause them to be uncontrollable." (75) "The more laws are enacted and taxes
assessed, the greater the number of law-breakers and tax-
evaders." (57) "When government governs little, people are
happy. When government governs much, people are miserable." (58)

Where government is necessary, what policy should be followed? "In managing men, or anything else, the intelligent
man uses self-restraint." (59) "Nature never acts, yet it activates everything. If legislators and administraters would behave likewise, each thing would develop in accordance with
its own nature." (37) "Whether governing a big country or
cooking a little fish, follow Nature's way and no evil tendencies will get control. This does not mean that the danger of
evils can be eliminated entirely, but only that they will cease
to harm men. When ordinary men are unharmed, their leaders are unharmed. And when nobody harms anybody, perfect
harmony prevails." (60) "The wise administrater does not
lead people to set their hearts upon what they cannot have,
but satisfies their inner needs. . . . He does not complicate
their lives with multifarious details or with an urge to attend
to this, that and the other. By keeping people contented, he
prevents those who mistakenly believe that ambition is better
than contentment from leading the contented astray." (3)

"A good leader guides by good example; a bad leader
resorts to force and intrigue." (57) "One's own individual life
serves as an example for other individuals. One's family life
serves as a model for other families. One's community serves
as a standard for other communities. One's state serves as a

measure for other states. And one's country serves as an ideal for all countries." (54) "The most intelligent leaders bring about results without making those controlled realize that they are being influenced. The less intelligent seek to motivate others by appeals to loyalty, honor, self-interest, and flattery. Those still less intelligent employ fear by making their followers think they will not receive their rewards. The worst try to force others to improve by condemning their conduct. But since, if leaders do not trust their followers, then their followers will not trust the leaders, the intelligent leader will be careful not to speak as if he doubted or distrusted his follower's ability to do the job suitably. When the work is done, and as he wanted it done, he will be happy if the followers say: 'This is just the way we wanted it.'" (17) "Intelligent control appears as uncontrol or freedom, and for that reason it is genuinely intelligent control. Unintelligent control appears as external domination. . . . Intelligent control exerts influence without appearing to do so. Unintelligent control tries to influence by making a show of force." (38)

"To be great, a state must be passively receptive, like the ocean which accepts whatever the rivers bring into it, or like the feminine which always submits to the masculine. . . . Thus a great state places itself at the service of a small state before it absorbs the small state. And the small state must serve the interests of the great state before it can be taken into the great state. Hence, some submit in order to take, while others submit in order to be taken. When a great state desires to have more people, and a small state desires to be protected, it is by submission that both obtain what they desire." (61)

War, as an instrument of public policy, is unwise, for "force will be met with force, and wherever force is used, fighting and devastation follows." (30) "Weapons have a negative value, for they create fear in others." (31) "The more weapons people possess, the more they fight." (57) Hence, "just as a fish should not be taken out of water, so a sword should never be taken from its scabbard." (36) However, when one is forced to use weapons, "he does so with reluctance and restraint." (31) "The best soldier does not attack. The superior fighter succeeds without violence. The greatest conquerer wins without a struggle." (68) "Military maxims say: 'It is easier to defend than to attack.' 'It is better to back away a foot than to assault to gain an inch.' This means that the best way to advance is to retreat. He who bares his flesh will appear to have no need for carrying weapons. He who does not flourish weapons, appears to have nothing to defend. He who does not prepare to defend himself appears to have no enemies. No one will attack a person unless he appears to be an enemy, for to attack one who is not an enemy is to lose a friend. Therefore, when opposing enemies meet for open battle, he who runs away to hide is the one who wins." (69) "The tougher fighters are more likely to be killed." (76) After a war is over, "he who is wise does not press a victory by further conquest. When peace has been restored, he does not behave like an arrogant victor. When security has been regained, he does not gloat like a conquerer. When he gets what he needs, he does not destroy those who have been defeated. Whenever he does something which he has to do, he does it without cruelty." (30) "There is a significant similarity between fighting and funerals. Just as a slaughter of many people should be accompanied by weeping and mourning, so the positions in a victory parade should properly parallel those in a funeral procession." (31)

Is Lao Tzu a Mystic?

Since Lao Tzu often has been called a mystic, by both appreciaters and scorners, and since mysticism is so generally misunderstood and mistrusted, some evaluation of his mysticism seems needed. First, three mistaken views must be rejected, namely, that his philosophy is difficult to understand, that it is similar to that of Hindu yogins, and that it is closely analogous to Christian mysticism. Then three ways in which he is mystical—ways in which all men, when they consider the matter, are, and must be, mystical—will be described.

Some claim that the philosophy of the *Tao Teh King* is incomprehensible. For whatever reason, e.g., haste or impatience with their failure to penetrate quickly into a philosophy alleged to be foreign, blindness due to narrow cultural loyalties or other intellectual precommittments, acquaintance with garbled texts or bungled translations, they have too quickly dismissed as worthless one of the simplest and clearest of the early philosophies of mankind. Despite translation difficulties (see final section of this commentary), the philosophy it expresses is elementary and universally recognizable as stating certain truths, even if not the whole truth, about life. Life itself is difficult to comprehend, but the *Tao Teh King* has simplified, perhaps over-simplified, its comprehension. The *Tao Teh King* is a classic of simplicity, not only of ancient China nor merely of Chinese civilization, but of all mankind for all time. The *Tao Teh King* belongs to humanity, and neither failures by literalistic etymologists nor claims by Chinese patriots to exclusive possession, can prevent world-wide appreciation of its universal spirit, at once both profound and simple, and both powerful and obvious.

A few (e.g., Blakney, pp. 35-37, Duyvendak, p. 11) suggest that Taoistic mysticism may be understood better if compared with Hindu mysticism. But any attempt to explain the one, which is extremely naturalistic, by the other, which is extremely spiritualistic, is bound to fail. If Lao Tzu had any interest in "ecstatic experience" (Blakney, p. 35), there is certainly nothing in the *Tao Teh King* to suggest it. Its theme is: accept what is natural. If one comes by ecstacy naturally, then why not? But to go in search of ecstacy for the sake of ecstasy would be considered artificial. It does not make ecstasy the goal of life. A life lived naturally is its own goal and needs no other. To take something other than life, or any part of life, as the goal of life, is to be misled. "If some part of him stands out as if a superior representative of his nature, he will not surrender the rest of his nature to it." (2, 10) Lao Tzu did not seek to shun society so that he might be undisturbed in pursuit of trances in "which the self was voided." (Blakney, p. 35) His central message advocated self-realization, and society was to be avoided only because, and to the extent that, it involved one person imposing himself upon other selves or being imposed upon by other selves. He prized individuality and despised even that partial voiding which comes from imposition. He was not interested in "ascetic practices" or "breathing exercises" (Duyvendak, p. 11) or "breath control" (Blakney, p. 36), because these are artificial attempts to redirect nature. Rather, "If you wish to live healthily, should you not breath naturally, like a child, and not hold your breath until your vitality is nearly exhausted?" (10) Breathing obviously exemplifies Nature's spontaneously alternating processes. Inhaling (yang) is followed automatically by exhaling (yin), and when the cycle is complete, it begins all over again. To hold one's breath is to try to force Nature to deviate from its course. Only evil can result. Lao Tzu was not a recluse seeking, like "any practiced sitting-thinker" (Blakney, p. 35), to hide away from nature. He accepted nature and wanted to live his own nature to the full. He sought to hide only from artificiality—artificiality in all its forms, including attempts to force oneself to sit, breath, or restrict desire in any unnatural way.

Those who prefer to interpret the mysticism of Lao Tzu as analogous to Christian mysticism risk misunderstanding due to looseness of analogy. Tao is not like God (See above pp. 76-78.) Furthermore, Western mystics, conceiving their union with God (See Blakney, p. 47) in the spirit of Western theological traditions, tend to think of such partial unity of self with God as they achieve in terms of a God who is other than, external to, or at least superior to, them. One must bridge a gap, transcend a distance, or at least rise above one's natural self, in order to unite with what is essentially other than one's natural self. But such mystical identity as appears in the *Tao Teh King,* being closer to Hindu than to Christian mysticism in this respect, finds the goal of his union already within himself, a union with Nature realized merely by being his natural self.

Turning to three varieties of mysticism present in the *Tao Teh King,* we shall discuss (1) intuition as a method of knowing, (2) feelings of identity of self with the universe, and (3) the ultimacy of mystery.

When intuiting, one accepts what appears as it appears, as self-evident, without wanting to explain it in terms of something else, something which does not appear. Intuition is direct or immediate apprehension, in contrast to indirect, mediate, hence inferential, apprehension. Explanation, deduction, inference—all these are attempts to interpret what appears, not in terms of itself, but in terms of something else, something external, something other than the thing itself. But if a knower is external to the thing known, he cannot know it as it is in itself. Hence he should accept the fact of his ignorance and not be deceived that he knows what he does not know. "The intelligent man is not deluded, because he knows and accepts his ignorance as ignorance, and thereby gains genuine knowledge." (71) The ultimate way to know is to be. Anything less than this identity of being and knowing erroneously mistakes a part for the whole, the abstract for the concrete, or the external (a description) for that which is internal (the thing described). "Nature can never be completely described, for such a description of Nature would have to duplicate Nature." (1) "Therefore the intelligent man accepts what is as it is. In seeking to grasp what is, he does not devote himself to making distinctions which are then mistaken for separate existences." (2) "In primitive times, intelligent men had an intuitively penetrating grasp of reality which could not be stated in words." (15) Lao Tzu was a mystic in recognizing the ultimacy of intuitive knowledge. But surely everyone who understands the nature of knowledge knows that whatever is mediated must reach its end in immediate apprehension. The data (i.e., sense data) upon which science rests are immediately apprehended. These simple data, apprehended without explanation, serve as the basis for explanation. In deduction, each step must be intuited, i.e., appear self-evident, before it is accepted. The universe as a whole is a self-sufficient and self-explanatory system which requires nothing external to account for it. Why interject non-self-explanatory principles into a system which is by nature, from beginning to end, self-explanatory? All other beings understand without explanation. Why should not man? Nature "does not explain; nevertheless all understand." (73) Lao Tzu is merely stating the obvious. If mysticism consists in direct apprehension of the obvious, then Lao Tzu is a mystic.

Feelings of identity of self with the universe, or my tao with Tao, also constitute a kind of mysticism and Lao Tzu was a mystic in this sense also. Tao is tao; tao is Tao. But the identity is not a mere identity, is not a reduction of taos to Tao, of parts to the whole, of many natures to one Nature. Nature is not "One." (Blakney, p. 29) Nature is both a unity and a plurality. Tao is constituted of taos. Each tao is nothing apart from Tao. Tao cannot separate itself from any of its taos. Yet neither collapses into the other. Lao Tzu's feeling of identity consists in feeling completely at home in the universe, or pluriverse, or unipluriverse, rather than, as with Advaita Vedanta, in feeling identical with a bare unity. The individual person, as a whole and with all of his parts, with his unity as a person and their (i.e., the parts) opposition to each other, is real, is the universe, is Tao, in action in this moment. Nature expresses itself not so much *through* persons (as means) as *in* persons (as ends). Each person is the universe (Tao) in action, and his being is Tao's doing, or his doing is Tao's being. Unity, if that means no division sliced by the law of excluded middle, is there; but plurality, each individual, each kind of animal, plant, or thing, and each stage in each life, is also ultimately real; for Tao is all of these things, not as a collection and not as a unity separable from the plurality, but as something which manifests itself as a unity through their plurality, as plural, as well. When one feels that he is what

he is as an integral part of the unipluriverse, his experience
is mystical; and who does not?

If "mystical" means "mysterious," then the *Tao Teh King*,
paradoxically, both does and does not advocate a mystical doctrine. It does, first of all, accept the fact that mystery is ever
present. Nature is "beyond comprehension and description."
(41) "Nature is the formless source of all forms. . . . Thus it
appears to us as if mysterious. No matter how closely we
scrutinize its coming toward us, we cannot discover a beginning. No matter how long we pursue it, we never find its end."
(14) "Nature is something which can be neither seen nor
touched." (21) "Since what is ultimate in Nature cannot be
seen with one's eyes, it is spoken of as invisible . . . inaudible
. . . intangible. But even all three of these together cannot adequately describe it. . . . If we cannot describe it intelligibly,
this is because it is beyond our understanding." (14) "If
Nature is inexpressible, he who desires to know Nature as it is
in itself will not try to express it in words." (1) "He who is
wise keeps silent." (56) But, on the other hand, the *Tao Teh
King* does not advocate mysteriousness. Ignorance is natural
and should be accepted as such. The irreproducibility of
Nature in any description of Nature is natural and should give
rise to no amazement. It is not the indescribability of Nature,
but the attempt to describe the undescribable, which is unnatural. One who accepts Nature for what it is has no experience
of mysteriousness. He feels no mystery. He fears no mystery.
Nature appears mysterious only to those who do not accept it
as it appears, and who thus desire to reconstruct and improve
upon Nature. Lao Tzu recognized the ultimacy of mystery for
those who wish to explain, but saw also that no mystery exists
for those accepting Nature's way. To explain means to inter-

pret something in terms of something else, something which it is not. Why should one want to interpret what is in terms of what it is not? Nature is self-sufficient. It needs no explanation and can have no explanation. One who accepts Nature as self-sufficient, and, therefore, as self-explanatory or self-evident, has no desire for explanation. What is self-evident is not mysterious. "Without looking out of his window, one can grasp the nature of everything." (47)

Lao Tzu and Confucius

The significance of the *Tao Teh King* may be more fully grasped by comparing its philosophy with that of Confucius. Both philosophies were not only among the earliest developed in Chinese history and foundational to all later philosophical thought in China, but also among the earliest developed by mankind anywhere and expressed certain fundamental ideals which have continued to be common to mankind everywhere. Their disagreements, which do in fact exist, have been over-emphasized by those wishing to differentiate between them. Leaving unprobed the perplexing problem of whether the men, Lao Tzu and Confucius, were contemporaries (and acquaintances, as one story has it) or which lived earlier, we may, nevertheless, point out that the ideals of Confucius pre-suppose many of the ideals expressed in the *Tao Teh King,* whereas the reverse is not true. The latter ideas appear more primitive, even if the dates of their formulation in a scholarly fashion remain uncertain. The philosophy of Confucius is more complicated, more developed, more sophisticated; the philosophy of Lao Tzu is more simple, more primary, more foundational. Their relationship is not that of two bitterly conflicting schools with diametrically opposed philosophies.

Confucius does not reject the foundations laid in the philosophy expressed by the *Tao Teh King,* but rejects the failure of Taoists to develop, on these foundations, further insights which are, in their way, equally important. To Confucius, the philosophy of Lao Tzu seems crude. To Lao Tzu, the philosophy of Confucius appears artificial. But neither, seen in its own light, can accept the derogatory judgment of the other.

In order to have a basis for comparison, we shall have to consider the philosophy of Confucius. It may be summarized by briefly examining the four complementary characteristics of the Ideal Man or Sage. In order to do so, we shall speak of *Yi, Jen, Li,* and *Chih.*

Yi is simply the best way of doing things, and an essential quality of the ideal man is that he understand Yi. Confucius, like Lao Tzu, presupposed that human nature is good; let it act naturally and all will go well. Hence, to let it act naturally is the best way of doing things. However, for Confucius, man is essentially and naturally social. Each man is born and raised in a family, marries, has a family of his own, and lives in a community where there are other families, and in a world where there are other communities. If man is naturally social, is there not also the nature (tao) of society? Yes, says Confucius, and he went in search, and spent a lifetime searching, for the tao of society, for the best way for men to behave in their social relations. Now Lao Tzu did not reject society (as did another Taoist, Yang Chu) but idealized the simplest rural society because here each individual least imposed upon, and was least imposed upon by, other persons. Confucius, on the other hand, accepting the fact that society exists and that people have to impose upon each other to a certain extent in order to live, even in the simplest family life, then sought those principles of social behavior which constitute the best ways of behaving—or the tao of society.

What are these principles? What happens when men act naturally? They marry and have children. When they do this they are naturally involved in certain relationships: husband-wife relationships and parent-child relationships. In fact, one cannot be born without coming into relationships with his own parents. Hence one is automatically involved in the problem of how to treat his parents and wife and child and of how he expects to be treated by them. Now if one will observe which kind of behavior begets what kinds of results, he will know what is the best way of treating his wife and child and parents. If he is rude or disrespectful, he will note that such rudeness is returned, oftentimes with interest. Hence he will discover that the principle of reciprocity is part of the tao of society. The best way of doing things, where others are involved, is to treat others as you would be treated if (and here the Confucian ideal involves a significant subtle addition to the usual Western formulation) you were in their shoes. This requires that one attempt to achieve some insight into how the other feels; or that one seek to comprehend the other's nature so as to understand how one would wish to be treated if he had that nature. It recognizes that each thing is good when it acts according to its own nature and that when one treats others he should not interfere with their nature by treating them as he would like to be treated (having his own nature) but as he would like to be treated if he had the nature of the other person. Hence, a father should treat his son as he would wish to be treated by his father if he were his son; and he should treat his father as he would like to be treated by his son if he were his father.

Now, although one may become convinced that this principle of reciprocity may be used to advantage in intimate family relations, does the same hold true regarding other social relations? Apparently many were not convinced, for Confucius took pains to elaborate that the principle holds also regarding all of the five fundamental relationships: parent-child, husband-wife, elder-younger brother, ruler-subject, and friend-friend. Furthermore, what holds for parents is extended to grandparents, great grandparents, and to departed ancestors, and what holds for friends of long-standing is extended to temporary guests and to strangers. Since, however, the way in which the principle works can be grasped most intuitively in the intimate child-parent relationship, "filial piety," as it is called, is the foundation for all the rest. And the ideal ruler governs his subjects, if not entirely by letting them follow their own natures uninhibited, at least as he would wish to be governed if he were one of his subjects. The ideal of governing by letting each man follow his own course is retained, but it is modified by taking into consideration the further principle of the best way of doing things when one is forced to impose himself (as a ruler must) upon others.

Another principle, called the "rectification of names," must be considered. Things, persons, officers, functions—all have names. Each kind of thing, each kind of social position, each kind of function, has its own kind of name. A parent is called a "parent," a wife is called a "wife," a ruler is called a "ruler." Now, surely, part of the best way of doing things is to call each thing by its right name. If a child is a child he should be called a "child" and not a "man." The principle of the rectification of names is another aspect of letting each thing act according to its own nature. Name and behavior should be correlated. If a thing has a name, i.e., one which distinguishes its nature or role or function, it should be permitted, and expected, to act accordingly. If it does not so act, it should not have that name; or that name does not rightly belong to it. If a wife runs about after other men, she no longer acts like a wife and, according to the principle of the rectification of names, should no longer be called, or treated like, a "wife." Not acting according to one's nature, and name, is to act artificially. Hence, the best way for a person to act is in accordance with his actual nature and right name. Of course, one must, also, accept his nature and act according to his name sincerely (Hsin); otherwise, as the principle of reciprocity dictates, he can expect to be dealt with insincerely by others.

Jen is good will. All individuals have some good will, but in the ideal man, good will becomes universal. Yet this is not a general, ambiguous, indifferent good will in which one wishes well to everyone while doing nothing for anyone. It is that kind of good will which is directed specifically to each person with whom one associates and which requires an effort to achieve sympathetic insight into his particular nature. Human nature is good, and each human being is good, and the nature (tao) of society is good when its principle of reciprocity is practiced. Jen is the willingness to treat others as ends in themselves; not only is it the willingness to let each person act in accordance with his own nature, but also the willingness to treat him as you would wish to be treated if you were he. Jen is the willingness to treat others in accordance with their own natures and names. This is the best way of doing things. Hence, in brief, Jen is the willingness to follow Yi. The ideal man not only understands Yi, but has the additional characteristic, Jen, the willingness to follow Yi.

Li is form. But it is form of many varieties and significations, including forms (essences as distinguished from matter or substance), uniformity (as in regularity and law), formality as in ceremonial behavior), and formalism (as when external expression no longer represents an underlying vitality). Confucius was interested in uniformities (much as scientists are today) discoverable regarding the tao of society. To find these he studied the regularly repeated behavior patterns prevailing in the various societies of his time. He travelled from society to society (kingdom to kingdom) as a scholar recording the persisting practices of people who succeeded in maintaining their positions in these societies. In any complex society, a division of labor requires that each function have its own functionary, its own name for that function, and its own methods, modes, or forms of procedure. Now these regular and uniform ways of procedure, being successful, must be the best ways or right ways, and they have come to be called right-uals or rituals. One who is skillful in the performance of his functions will seek (like scientists today) to be rigorous, precise, exact, in repeating his performance of any regular function. The more careful, the more precise, he is regarding each point of procedure, the more he may be called "punctilious." The principle of rectification of names, which is part of the best way of doing things, implies that performance of functions named is most right when it is most precise. For example, if one is a son, surely there is a way of behaving which will best express one's sonship, or if one is a teacher, surely there is a most effective way of teaching. Now that way is Li.

However, Li must be distinguished from Yi, which is also the best way of doing things. The difference between Yi and Li, at least relative to characterizing the ideal man, corresponds to the difference between inner and outer. That is, Yi is the best way of doing things when a thing or person acts according to its own inner nature, or when a person within society acts in accordance with the tao of society. Li is the way in which inner action manifests itself in external appearances and behavior patterns. For each Yi, or best inner way of behaving, there is an appropriate Li, or best outer manner of expressing that way. Yi and Li should always go together fittingly. If they do not, if the external manner is improper or does not express the inner feelings and motives, it is false. Hence, the principle of the rectification of names is violated. Formalism, conformity to external forms which do not properly express the intent, is to be avoided. If later Confucians, like later adherents to most stable (hence static) cultural ideals, mistook formalistic ritualism for Confucianism, the fault is theirs, not that of Confucius. The Confucian ideal man knows and practices Li in accordance with the principle of the rectification of names.

Chih is wisdom. It is not that kind of wisdom which requires a knowledge of many facts, but the kind which consists in actual achievement of contentment and in enjoyment of profound confidence. Wisdom is not a momentary affair; one wisecrack does not make one a wise man. Wisdom involves enduring happiness, and no man is wise until he is happy. Wisdom consists in wanting what is best, both for oneself and others, both internally and externally. Hence wisdom involves a willingness to act in accordance with Yi and Jen and Li. Now this willingness might be achieved momentarily, and then forgotten. But Chih, wisdom, arrives only as one achieves such willingness completely and continuingly. When willingness is thus complete, it turns itself into habits of acting without reservation when faced with the question of deciding whether or not to act according to Yi, Jen and Li. One's behavior conforms automatically and spontaneously with the tao of society. Complete intellectual honesty, complete genuine good will, and complete moral spontaneity, are all essential to the ideal man in whom the tao of society is most perfectly embodied. That such an ideal must remain an ideal, seldom if ever realized, is suggested by the fact that Confucius himself complained that he himself had never attained it. Yet this ideal stands as one of the greatest, one of the most profoundly inspiring, ever conceived by man.

Having summarized the philosophy of Confucius, perhaps so briefly as to have risked serious omission and distortion, let us compare it with that of Lao Tzu.

First of all, many similarities are obvious. Both accepted and expressed a common naturalistic and humanistic tradition, sharing a common language and common basic concepts, such as Tao, Yang, Yin, used in interpreting both Nature at large and human nature. Both accepted the same general cosmology, with its cyclical theory of change, its natural orderliness: each thing beginning, waxing to its fullness, waning, and disappearing, all in accordance with its own inner nature. Both accepted Nature at large and also human nature as good, so long as things followed their natural course; but both admitted, and advised how to deal with, the evils arising from deviation from that course. Both recognized as fundamental a distinction between the inner and outer and considered the inner more basic. Both idealized spontaneity as essential to wisdom. Both objected to the use of force in influencing others, especially in government, and both advocated appeal to each man's own interests, or inner nature, as the best method of governing. Both agreed that the best way to control others is by example and that "the ideal state is one which has a sage at its head."[19] Both were scholars (Confucius "a collector of the wisdom of the ancients," Lao Tzu "a keeper of the royal archives") and teachers (judging by their reputations), rather than rulers, warriors, farmers, or merchants. Both sought and taught others to seek what is vital, ultimate, genuine, and to shun the merely formal, artificial, and external.

Secondly, their differences' appear to be primarily those of degree, arising naturally out of differences in the locus of their interests and focus of their efforts. Both were naturalistic and humanistic, but Lao Tzu felt man to be more genuinely human and natural when enjoying a rural life uncomplicated by regulations, taxes, and their enforcement, while Confucius accepted the social as just as natural as the rural and men as genuinely human in association with others as in relative isolation. Both recognized Nature's rituals, the regular sequences of day and night, the seasons, birth and death, as following an inner course with which one should not interfere. But Lao Tzu saw such natural process as wholly inner or as wholly self-sufficient within each particular being, whereas Confucius saw the interactions between such beings as also part of the natural processes and to be recognized, accepted, and studied as such. Neither appealed to a God or any other principle outside the process. But Lao Tzu saw in the social the chief source of deviations from Nature's way, whereas Confucius, beginning by presupposing the social as an ancient aspect of Nature, devoted himself to understanding the social area of Nature's way so as to avoid the evils of deviations therein.

Regarding how to deal with social problems, i.e., where

[19] Fung Yu-lan, *A Short History of Chinese Philosophy*, p. 102.

people impose upon one another, Lao Tzu would prefer, first of all, to avoid unnecessary association with others, by staying at home away from even his nearest neighbors; then, to own nothing which others might want to take from him, to humble himself so no one would wish to compete with him, and to disarm himself so no one will wish to fight with him; then, whenever he has a surplus, to give to others, even though he gets nothing in return; and finally, when trouble arises anyway, to run away and hide until the conflict is over, and leave others alone even when they do not leave him alone. Confucius, on the other hand, idealized, not running away, but reciprocity which, together with rectification of names, provides assurance for social harmony. If men will but treat each other justly, or properly, there will be no need for running away. If one's society assures him that his own nature, as recognized by his correct name, will be respected, he need have nothing to fear. Of course, when people deviate from these principles, trouble results. Although effort to achieve sympathetic insight is required by the principle of reciprocity, for Confucius this comes naturally when people are intimately associated. Lao Tzu's profound confidence that Nature's way is sufficient to provide complete self-development for each person required no special effort at insight in order to express his beneficence. When, reciprocally, each leaves the other alone, all the values claimed for the principle of reciprocity are automatically fulfilled. But, for Confucius, people cannot associate by leaving each other alone; since they do and must associate, understanding and practice of reciprocity, sympathetic insight, and right names (Yi, Jen, and Li) are requisites —something to be faced rather than run away from.

Although both idealized spontaneity as essential to wisdom,

Lao Tzu saw whatever principles were embodied in the self-activity with which Nature endowed each person as wholly sufficient, needing no supplementation by external principles. Each man is wisest when he follows his own inner nature uninfluenced by anything external. But, for Confucius, what is inner expresses itself in outer behavior, and the inner and outer are correlative to each other, every Yi having its Li, and every Li its Yi. Hence attention to outer form of Nature's inner ritual is equally desirable, especially in social situations where what is external is most obvious to others. However, he admits that not until one has achieved Chih, wherein one accepts what is to be done, outer as well as inner (Yi, Jen, Li), habitually, automatically, unquestioningly, and hence spontaneously, does one achieve wisdom. Only when one is as completely at home in society, and as spontaneously social, as Lao Tzu's ideal man is spontaneously natural in rural isolation, has he arrived at Confucian wisdom. When Yi, Jen, Li, and Chih have become embodied in one's self, then one is self-actively, self-sufficiently, spontaneously social.

Although both idealized ruling by example, for Lao Tzu, Nature's own example of guiding without external interference is sufficient example, whereas, for Confucius, only a leader who embodies Yi, Jen, Li and Chih is ideal. Two further items should be noticed about Confucius' view. First, "when a sage becomes a ruler, he should do many things for the people, whereas according to the Taoists, the duty of the sage ruler is not to do things, but rather to undo or not to do at all."[20] Secondly, use of force is permissible, according to the principle of reciprocity, for when one is attacked, he may be

[20] *Ibid.*

expected to retaliate; reciprocity permits return of evil for evil as well as good for good.

Hence, finally, it must be admitted that some genuine differences between the philosophies of Lao Tzu and Confucius exist, even though they grew out of a common cultural tradition and began as differences in degree. The social tends to be artificial for Lao Tzu but natural for Confucius. The inner is self-sufficient for Lao Tzu whereas inner and outer are correlative for Confucius and hence attention to ritual is required. Reciprocity is not necessary for Lao Tzu for, like Nature, one who has more than enough for himself should give to others even though he receives nothing in return, while Confucius believes that perfection of reciprocity, conceived in terms of requiring insight into each other's nature and wishes, is essential to a perfect society. For Lao Tzu, living in the present, whether from day to day or year to year, is enough; one should not, like Confucius, search into the practices of men of the past, whose bones have long since decayed, for to impose the natures of dead men upon living men is even worse, perhaps, than present men imposing upon each other; Confucius, on the other hand, exhibiting the universal interest of a scientist, sought universal behavior patterns, past as well as present, in other kingdoms as well as in his own. A final difference, which some may consider most important, has to do with the use of names: Since the principle of rectification of names is so fundamental for Confucius, he has to be interested in the names of things and distinctions between names; but Lao Tzu, believing that Tao is, ultimately, indescribable and unnamable, thought of names as external, and hence artificial, impositions, and thus condemned the interest in names and naming and in making distinctions between names and then naming the distinctions.

However, despite these differences, one must utterly reject Cheng Lin's view that the philosophy of the Taoist school, at least as expressed in the *Tao Teh King,* "is so opposite to the Chinese mind that its indigenous origin is doubted." (Cheng Lin, p. 7.) Although he is not prepared to substantiate it, the writer nevertheless favors the view of Lin Yutang that "among scholars who know the Orient, there are more devotees of Laotse than of Confucius." (Lin Yutang, p. 3.)

Translation Difficulties

Perhaps the most intriguing fact about the *Tao Teh King* is the power is has over the minds of its readers to demand further interpretation. It is the "most translated of all Chinese texts" (Lin Yutang, p. 3), appearing in at least forty English translations to date, and promises to be translated many times more. "For one reason or another, each translation, in its turn, fails fully to satisfy one who knows the original, and at length, one tries his own hand at it." (Blakney, p. 9.) But, in addition, one can never know the original, which is lost in history, but only one or more of the at least "eighty-three different editions" in Chinese.[21] "From the Hann Dynasty to the end of the Manchu Dynasty no less than 335 annotated editions have been listed. All old editions have this in common: the text is replete with typographical errors and later interpolations." (Cheng Lin, p. 6.) "The Chinese themselves...are almost unanimous in denying its authenticity." (Giles, p. 10.) "The Chinese system of writing had undergone a number of changes

[21] See Shih-Hsiang Chen, in *Literature East and West,* Spring, 1955, Vol. II, No. 1, p. 17.

between the earliest times and the third century B.C.," and "until very recently no punctuation was used in Chinese writing, and such ambiguities as abound in classical syntax may easily result in different readings. . . . Few editors or translators have ever been able to resist the temptation of 'touching up' the text to accord with the result of their own researches." (Ch'u Ta-Kao, pp. 5-7.) "There can be little doubt that any translation from the Chinese is capable of extreme flexibility and license, of which, indeed, the translator must avail himself if he would rightly render the spirit rather than the letter of the text; and the spirit, after all, is the essential thing, if we follow the teaching of Laotze. It is safe to say that the more literal the translation may be the more obscure its meaning." (Old, p. 19.)

BIBLIOGRAPHY

Twelve English editions of the *Tao Teh King* were used in preparing the present interpretation. One of these, that by Witter Bynner, a fellow New Mexican, has served as an example for interpreting the *Tao Teh King* without direct reference to Chinese texts.[22] Although greatly admiring Bynner's work, especially for its profound grasp, terse expression, and poetic style, the writer rejects the ideal that Lao Tzu's extreme naturalism provided any place for poetry. Despite the presence of rhymes in early Chinese texts, neither rhyming nor metaphorical subtlety are essential to the doctrine or its mode of expression. Later Taoists explicitly criticized followers of Confucius for wasting time on music and poetry.

The twelve editions are:

G. G. Alexander, "Tao-Teh-King" or "Book of the Values of Tao," *Sacred Books and Early Literature of the East,* Vol. XII, p. 15-31. Parke, Austin and Lipscomb, Inc., New York and London, 1917 (1895).

R. B. Blakney, *The Way of Life: Lao Tsu.* The New American Library (Mentor Book 129), New York, 1955.

Witter Bynner, *The Way of Life According to Lao-Tsu.* John Day, New York, 1944.

Ch'u Ta-Kao, *Tao Tê Ching.* The Buddhist Society of London, London, 1937, 1948.

[22] Two other examples, editions by Old and Ould (see final list), are cited by Holmes Welch, *The Parting of the Way,* p. 17.

J. J. L. Duyvendak, *Tao Te Ching: The Book of the Way and Its Virtue.* John Murray, London, 1954.

Lionel Giles, *The Sayings of Lao Tzŭ.* John Murray, London, 1905, 1950.

Dwight Goddard and Bhikshu Wai-Tao, "Tao-Teh-King," *A Buddhist Bible,* Second Edition, pp. 407-436. Dwight Goddard, Thetford, Vermont, 1938 (1936).

Ernest R. Hughes, "Tao Te Ching," *Chinese Philosophy in Classical Times,* pp. 141-164. J. M. Dent and Sons (Everyman Library 973), London, 1942, 1950.

James Legge, "Tao-Teh King," *Sacred Books and Early Literature of the East,* Vol. XII, pp. 32-74. Parke, Austin and Lipscomb, New York and London, 1917 (1891).

Lin Yutang, *The Wisdom of Laotse.* Random House (Modern Library 262), New York, 1948.

Isabella Mears, *Tao Teh King.* Theosophical Publishing House London, Ltd., London, 1916, 1949.

Arthur Waley, *The Way and Its Power.* G. Allen and Unwin, London, 1934, 1949.

The works of seven other translaters were used during the preparation of the Comments. These are:

Paul Carus, *The Canon of Reason and Virtue.* Open Court Publishing Co., La Salle, Ill., 1898, 1913, 1937.

Cheng Lin, *The Works of Lao Tzyy: Truth and Nature.* World Book Co., Ltd., Taipei, Taiwan, 1953.

Dwight Goddard, *Laotzu's Tao and Wu Wei,* with an interpretation by Henri Borel. Brentano's, New York, 1919.

Walter Gorn Old, *The Simple Way, Laotze.* Philip Wellby, London, 1904, 1905.

E. H. Parker, *Studies in Chinese Religion,* pp. 96-131. E. P. Dutton, New York, and Chapman and Hall, London, 1910 (1903).

The Simple Way of Lao Tsze. The Shrine of Wisdom, Fintry, Brook, Godalming, Surry, England, 1924, 1941, 1951.

Sum Nung Au-Young, *Lao Tze's Tao Teh King.* March and Greenwood, Publishers, New York, 1938.

Finally, for those curious about the history of English translations, the following list, chronologically arranged, is appended. The writer has depended heavily upon a bibliography assembled by Clark Melling whose lifelong collection of editions, translations into English and other languages, and commentaries on Lao Tzu is one of the best. It is included in the Special Collections of the University of New Mexico's Zimmerman Library, where he served as a librarian during most of his life.

1868 John Chalmers, *The Speculations on Metaphysics, Polity and Morality of "The Old Philosopher," Lau-tsze.* Trubner, London.

1884 Frederick Henry Balfour, *Taoist Texts, Ethical, Political and Speculative.* Kelly and Walsh, Shanghai; Trubner, London.

1886 Herbert A. Giles, "The Remains of Lao Tzu," *China Mail,* Vol. XIV, pp. 231-280. Hongkong.

1891 James Legge, "Tao-Teh King," *Sacred Books of the East,* Vol. XXXIX, pp. 47-124, Oxford University Press, London; *Sacred Books and Early Literature of the East,* Vol. XII, pp. 32-74, Parke, Austin and Lipscomb, New York and London, 1917.

1894 Walter Gorn Old, *The Book of the Path of Virtue,* or a Version of the Tao Teh King of Lao-tsze. Theosophical Publishing Society, Madras.

1895 G. G. Alexander, *Lao-tsze, The Great Thinker,* with a Translation of His Thoughts on Nature and Manifestations of God. Kegan Paul, Trench, Trubner, London; "Tao-Teh-King" or "Book of the Values of Tao," *Sacred Books and Early Literature of the East,* Vol. XII, pp. 15-31, Parke, Austin and Lipscomb, Inc., New York and London, 1917.

1896 Paul Carus, "Lao-Tsze's Tao-Teh-King," *The Monist,* Vol. VII, pp. 571-601; Laotze's *Tao-Teh-King.* Open Court Publishing Co., Chicago, 1898.

1898 P. J. Maclagen, "The Tao Teh King," *The China Review,* Vol. XXIII, pp. 1-14, 75-85, 125-142, 191-207, 261-264; Vol. XXIV, pp. 12-20, 86-92.

1899 T. W. Kingsmill, "Tao Teh King," *Shanghai Mercury; The China Review,* Vol. XXIV, pp. 149-155, 185-194.

1903 E. H. Parker, "Tao Teh King," *The Dublin Review,* July, 1903, and January, 1904; E. H. Parker, *China and Religion,* pp. 271-301, Dutton, New York, 1905; *Studies in Chinese Religion,* pp. 96-131, Dutton, New York, and Chapman and Hall, London, 1910.

1903 I. W. Heysinger, *Light of China, The Tao Teh King of Lao T'sze.* Peter Reilly, Philadelphia; Research Publishing Co., Philadelphia.

1904 Lionel Giles, *The Sayings of Lao Tzŭ.* John Murray, London, 1905, 1950.

1904 Walter Gorn Old, *The Simple Way, Laotze, The "Old Boy,"* A New Translation of the Tao-Teh-King. Philip Wellby, London; Rider, London; McKay, Philadelphia.

1905 C. Spurgeon Medhurst, *Tao Teh King,* A short Study in Comparative Religion. Theosophical Society, Chicago.

1911 Carl Henrik Andreas Bjerregaard, *The Inner Life and the Tao-Teh King.* Theosophical Publishing House, London; The Theosophical Publishing Co. of New York, New York.

1913 Paul Carus, *The Canon of Reason and Virtue* (a second translation). Open Court Publishing Co., La Salle, Ill., 1913, 1937, 1954.

1916 Isabella Mears, *Tao Teh King.* Theosophical Publishing House, London, 1916, 1922, 1949.

1919 Dwight Goddard and Henri Borel, *Lao Tsu's Tao and Wu Wei.* Brentano's New York.

1920 A. E. Anderson, "The Tao Teh King; A Chinese Mysticism," *University Chronicle,* Vol. XXII, pp. 395-403, University of California, Berkeley.

1923 J. G. Weis, *Lao-Tze's Tao-Teh-King.* Typewritten copy in British Museum, London.

1924 *The Simple Way of Lao Tsze.* The Shrine of Wisdom, Fintry, Brook, Godalming, Surry, England, 1924, 1941, 1951.

1926 Charles Henry Mackintosh. *Tao.* Theosophical Press, Chicago.

1926 Wu-wu-tze and L. P. Phelps, *The Philosophy of Lao-tzu.* Modern Industrial Society, Jeh Hsin Press, Chengtu, Szechuan, China.

1927 T. MacInnes, *The Teachings of the Old Boy.* J. M. Dent, Toronto.

1928 Shuten Inouye, *Laotse, Tao Teh King.* Daitokaku, Tokoyo.

1934 Arthur Waley, *The Way and Its Power.* George Allen and Unwin, London.

1935 Ch'en Ku-ying, *Lao Tzu* (translated and adapted by Rhett Y. W. Young and Roger T. Ames). Chinese Materials Center, San Francisco. ????

1936 Hu Tse-ling, *Lao Tzu, Tao Teh Ching.* Canadian Mission Press, Chengtu, Szechwan.

1936 Bhikshu Wai Tao and Dwight Goddard, "Tao-Teh-King," *A Buddhist Bible.* Dwight Goddard, Thetford, Vermont; Second edition, 1938, pp. 407-437.

1936 A. L. Kitselman II, *Tao teh king (The Way of Peace) of Lao Tzu.* The School of Simplicity, Palo Alto, California.

1937 Ch'u Ta-Kao, *Tao Tê Ching.* The Buddhist Society of London, 1937, 1942, 1948.

1938 Sum Nung Au-young, *Lao Tzu's Tao Teh King,* the Bible of Taoism. March and Greenwood, New York.

1939 Hu Tse-Ling, *Lao Tsu Tao Teh Ching.* Cheng-tu, Szechuan, China.

1939 (John) Wu Ching-Hsiung, "Lao Tzu's The Tao and Its Virtue," *T'ien Hsia Monthly,* Nov., 1939, pp. 401-423, Dec., 1939, pp. 498-521, Jan., 1940, pp. 66-69, Shanghai; *Journal of Oriental Literature,* Vol. 4 (1951), pp. 2-33, Oriental Literature Society, University of Hawaii, Honolulu.

1942 Ernest R. Hughes, "Tao Te Ching," *Chinese Philosophy in Classical Times,* pp. 144-164. J. M. Dent and Sons (Everyman Library 973), London.

1942 Lin Yutang, "The Wisdom of Laotse," *Wisdom of India and China,* pp. 583-624, Random House, New York; *The Wisdom of Laotse,* Random House (Modern Library 262), New York, 1948.

1944 Witter Bynner, *The Way of Life According to Lao Tsu.* John Day, New York.

1945 Eduard Erkes, "Ho-Shang-Kung's Commentary on Lao Tse," *Artibus Asiae,* Vol. VIII (1945), pp. 119-196, Vol. IX

(1946), pp. 197-220, Vol. XII (1949), pp. 221-251. Ascona, Switzerland.

1946 Herman Ould, *The Way of Acceptance,* A New Version of Lao Tse's Tao te ching. A. Dakers, London.

1948 Frederick B. Thomas, *The Tao Teh of Laotse.* Oakland, California.

1949 Orde Poynton, *The Great Sinderesis,* being a translation of the Tao Te Ching. The Hassell Press, Adelaide, Australia.

1949 Cheng Lin, *The Works of Lao Tzyy, Truth and Nature,* popularly known as Daw-Der-Jing by Lao Dan. World Publishers, Shanghai; The World Book Co., Ltd., Taipei, Taiwan, 1953.

1954 Jan Julius Lodewijk Duyvendak, *Tao Te Ching: The Book of the Way and Its Virtue.* John Murray, London.

1955 R. B. Blakney, *The Way of Life: Lao Tsu.* The New American Library (Mentor Book 129), New York.

1959 Sohaku Ogata, *Zen for the West* (Appendix: *A Zen Interpretation of the Tao Te Ching*). Dial Press, New York.

1961 Leon Hurvitz, translation of *A Recent Japanese Study of Lao-Tzu* by Eiichi Kimura. *Monumenta Sinica,* Vol. 20, pp. 311-367, The Catholic University of Nagoya.

1961 John C. Wu, *Lao Tzu. Tao Teh King.* St. John's University Press, New York.

1962 Frank J. MacHovac, *The Book of Tao.* Peter Pauper, Mount Vernon, New York.

1963 D. C. Lau, *Tao Te Ching.* Chinese University Press, Hong Kong.

1963 Wing-Tsit Chan, *The Way of Lao Tzu.* Bobbs-Merrill, Indianapolis.

1967 Chang Chi-chun (Constant C. C. Chang) and William Forthman, *Lao Tzu.* Meredith Publishing Company, New York.

1968 Ko Lien-hsiang, *Commentaries on Lao Tzu's Tao Te Ching.* L. H. Ke, Taipei.

1969 Tang Zi-chang, *Wisdom of Dao.* T. C. Press, San Rafael, California.

1970 Constant C. C. Chang, *Wisdom of Taoism.* Bulletin of National Taiwan University, Vol. XV, June, 1970, pp. 241-386.

1970 T. H. Yu, *The Philosophy of Taoism.* Falcon Publishers, San Francisco.

1971 Bennett Sims, *Lao-Tzu and the Tao Te Ching.* Franklin Watts, New York.

1972 A. Roger Home, *The Great Art of Laotse.* Newbard House, Exeter.

1972 Feng Gia-fu and Jane English, *Tao Te Ching/Lao Tzu.* Knopf, New York.

1975 Alan Watts and Al Chung-Liang Huang, *Tao: The Watercourse Way.* Pantheon, New York.

1975 Chang Chung-yuan, *Tao: A New Way of Thinking.* Harper and Row, New York.

1975 Aleister Crowley, *The Tao Teh King.* Thelema Publications, Kings Beach, California.

1975 Bernhard Karlgren, *Notes on Lao Tzu. The Museum of Far Eastern Antiquities Bulletin,* No. 47, pp. 1-18, Stockholm.

1975 Karl Otto Schmidt, *Tao-Teh-Ching: Lao Tzu's Book of Life* (translated from German by Leone Muller). CSA Press, Lakemont, Georgia.

1976 Yen Ling-feng, *A Reconstructed Lao Tzu,* translated from Chinese by Chu Ping-yi and edited by Ho Kuang-mo. Ch'eng Wen Publishing Co., Taipei.

1977 Y. T. Hsuing, *Lao Tze, Tao Te Ching. Chinese Culture.* Vol. 18, June, 1977, pp. 1-48. Institute for Advanced Studies, China Academy, Taiwan.

1977 Paul J. Lin, *A Translation of Lao Tzu's Tao Te Ching and Wang Pi's Commentary. Michigan Papers in Chinese Studies,* No. 30, Center for Chinese Study, University of Michigan, Ann Arbor.

1977 Rhett Y. W. Young and Roger T. Ames, *Lao Tzu: Text, Notes and Comments,* by Ch'en Ku-ging. Chinese Materials Center, San Francisco.

1979 Ju-Chou Yang and Edward K. Chook, *Lao Tzyy Dow Der Jing.* Taipei.

1979 Ni Hua-ching, *The Complete Works of Lao Tzu: Tao Teh Ching*

& *Hua Hu Ching*. Shrine of the Eternal Breath of Tao, Malibu, California.

1979 Ariane Rump in collaboration with Wing Tsit Chan, *Commentary on the Lao Tzu by Wang Pi*. University of Hawaii Press, Honolulu.

1980 Lao C'en, *The Way of the Dao: An Interpretation of the Writings of Lao Tzu*. Day Press, La Jolla.

1980 John R. Leebrick, *Tao Teh Ching: Classic of the Way and Its Nature*. Afterimage Book Publishers, Urbana, Illinois.

1981 Man-jan Cheng, *Lao-Tzu* (translated by Tam C. Gibbs). North Atlantic Books, Richmond, California.

1981 Benjamin Hoff, *The Way to Life at the Heart of the Tao Te Ching* (selections adapted from various translations). Weatherhill, New York.

1982 Herrymon Maurer, *Tao: The Way of the Ways*. Schocken Books, New York.

1982 Tolbert McCarroll, *The Tao: The Sacred Way*. Crossroad, New York.

1982 Henry Wei, *The Guiding Light of Lao Tzu*. Theosophical Publishing House, Wheaton, Illinois.

1983 Raghaven Iyer, *Tao Te Ching. Lao Tzu*. Concord Grove Press, Santa Barbara, California.

1984 Leon Weiger, *The Wisdom of the Daoist Masters,* translated from French of Leon Weiger's *Les Peres du Systeme Taoiste* by Derek Bryce. Llanerch Enterprises, Llanerch, Felinbach, Lampeter, Dyfed, Wales.

1985 John Heider, *The Tao of Leadership: Lao Tzu's Tai Te Ching, Adapted for a New Age*. Humanics New Age, Atlanta, Georgia.

1985 Richard Wilhelm, *Tao Te Ching: The Book of Meaning and Life,* translated from German by H. G. Ostwald. Routledge and Kegan Paul, London.

1986 R. L. Wing, *The Tao of Power*. Doubleday, Garden City, New York.

1988 Liu I-Ming, *Awakening to the Tao* (tr. by Thomas Clearly). Shambala Publications, Boston.

1988 Stephen Mitchell, *Tao Te Ching*. Harper and Row, New York.

1989 Ellen M. Chen, *The Tao Te Ching*. Paragon House, New York.

1989 Robert G. Henricks, *Lao-Tzu Te-Tao Ching*. Ballantine Books, New York.

1989 Yi Wu, *The Book of Lao Tzu*. Great Learning Publishing Company, San Francisco.

1990 Victor H. Mair, *Tao Te Ching: The Classic Book of Integrity and The Way*. Bantam Books, New York.

1990 John C. H. Wu, *Tao Te Ching*. Shambala. Boston.

1991 Alan K. Chan, *Two Visions of The Way. A Study of the Wang Pi and the Ho-Shang Kung Commentaries on the Lao-Tzu*. SUNY Press, Albany.

1991 Stephen Mitchell, *Tao Te Ching*. Harper Collins, New York.

1992 Michael LaFargue, *The Tao of the Tao Te Ching*. SUNY Press, Albany.

1992 Thomas H. Miles, *Tao Te Ching: About the Way of Nature and Its Powers*. Avery Publishing Group, Garden City Park.

1992 Leon Weiger, *Tao Te Ching. Lao Zi*. Llanerch Publishers, Llanerch, Wales.

ACKNOWLEDGMENTS

The writer is endebted to Witter Bynner, Carsun Chang, H. G. Creel, Sang-Eun Lee and Y. P. Mei for comments on the manuscript and especially to Wing-tsit Chan for detailed critical remarks which resulted in improvements in both text and comments, to Clark Melling for assistance with the bibliography, to Hubert Alexander and Luna Bahm for improvements in style, to the University of New Mexico and its Research Committee for funds for circulating the manuscript to critics, and to Longmans, Green and Co., and other publishers as indicated in the footnotes, for permission to quote from their publications.

The book was published by Frederick Ungar Publishing Company, New York, 1958–1985, with fourteen printings, and by Crossroad-Continuum, New York, 1985–1992. Revisions in the Second Edition published by World Books, Albuquerque, consist primarily in extending the list of English translations from 1955 to 1989.

The book was reprinted in *The Collection of the Conference Papers* of the Second World Conference on Taoism held in Taipei, September 9-17, 1990, sponsored by The International Society for Taoism.